TABLE OF CONTENTS

PREFACE

The last several years of my personal and professional life have been extremely challenging. We were told to go to school, get a decent degree, a suitable job and life would be great! However, in reality the process of following this cookie-cutter plan was easier said than done and not as rewarding as it was supposed to be.

My journey started in Libreville, Gabon in Africa. Then from Africa to Marmande, France, where I grew up. Early in my twenties, I moved to Ireland. A place where I didn't know anyone or even the language to complete my MBA and to start my professional career in corporate finance. Several work opportunities with different multinational organizations led me from Dublin to New York, to Singapore, to Los Angeles and now to Chicago, which is currently home. There was no straight line from my very humble beginnings to the corner office or a six-figure salary.

Being a millennial, raised by Generation X and managed by Baby Boomers at work, my career and life path have taught me some very significant lessons. Not to mention the fact that I've also lived through an incredible amount of suffering. I know firsthand how it is to be and go without. I know how it feels to be at the bottom and feel humiliated but still have to keep a straight face and pretend to be unaffected. There have been times in my life when I had nothing to eat, times when I appeared to be successful, but in reality, I was struggling and on my last. I knew the truth, even if no one else could see it.

I've had to fight through and overcome feelings of abandonment, struggles with personal identity, low self-esteem, depression, financial and career struggles, loneliness, the feeling of being lost and not knowing what to do with my life, the fear of people wanting to maliciously hurt me, getting lost in my own internal chatter, and not feeling deserving of love and happiness.

All these challenges throughout my life led me to

have a lot of self-doubt, negative thoughts, debilitating inner criticism and they caused me to experience a great deal of internal and external misery. Many times, I simply wanted to give up! I can affirm that it has been hell at times.

On many occasions, I asked myself, "Is this what my life is supposed to be? What will it take for me to be successful and happy?" One night at home, sitting at my kitchen table, I wondered, "What is my purpose in life? Is this life supposed to only be about waking up every day, commuting for 50 minutes to work, and enduring never-ending challenges? Was I supposed to repeat this mundane routine for 30 years, retire, get old, and die? It couldn't be! There must be a way to play in this game of life successfully," I thought.

I concluded that there had to be ways for each person on the planet to fully understand and embrace what it takes to win at life on their respective paths. I was determined to figure out the ways. Once I did, I promised myself that I would share my findings with others. Since that night I've spent a significant amount of time, energy, and money gaining specific knowledge and learning in-depth about the power of self-awareness, spirituality, scientific knowledge on human behavior, and business process information.

Thanks to all of my difficult experiences and tough questions, along with the signs that the Universe gave me, and the conscious investment in my personal development, I've learned the many skills which helped me turn what seemed to be challenges, curses, and never-ceasing pain into blessings and success.

I've been able to end my own personal suffering by learning that the Universal God is protecting, guiding, and leading me. I came to realize that I'm not alone on this journey. By accepting this reality, a lot of pressure, sadness, and self-inflicted solitude was alleviated. Once I realized the highest and biggest power, *All,* is with me every day, every moment, I was able to release a lot of fear and self-limiting beliefs. I also learned that the key to receiving is *asking.*

All I needed to do was ask and seek the Universal God's guidance. Once I began to inquire about what my purpose was and look for the answers to specific questions to improve my life, the answers came. This was a really, really powerful catalyst for a change in perspective for me.

Learning the various techniques considered "secret" somehow in our society opened doors as well. These techniques include: neuro-linguistic programming (NLP), the importance of understanding personality types, emotional intelligence, the art of communication, negotiation and compensation, talk-therapy, self-hypnosis, and meditation are all skills that have helped me to master my mind and navigate through life with more success and fulfillment. On my path to enlightened success and fulfillment, I had the opportunity and eventually the resources to learn from some of the best teachers throughout the world.

However, many people that struggle in life and deal with a lot of the same issues I had to face and overcome are the most in need of this critical knowledge, but more-than-likely not able to access this life-transforming information. Either they don't have the time or the resources to invest in finding the keys to access their innate wealth.

The good news is that they don't have to and neither do you. This book is my attempt to keep the promise I made to myself all those years ago at my kitchen table. I've taken all of my years of learning and condensed them into five critical areas or universal principles that will help you unlock transformation in your life. The purpose of this book is to share with you a holistic, practical, no nonsense blueprint to equip you with the powerful tools you can use right away to thrive in your personal and professional life.

Success doesn't just apply to money either. Although the energy of money is an essential, beautiful energy to understand and master in order to achieve and realize our dreams, it is only one pillar of success. If you're not healthy mind, body, and spirit, all the money in the world won't matter. It's absolutely vital to aim at succeeding in all these areas collectively. Too often we try to separate everything and act as if we don't need them all. Good health, spirituality, and monetary wealth are all essential components of a fulfilling life. We should aim to create and maintain harmony and balance in all areas, at all times.

Only being wealthy or influential pale in comparison to taking action to make this world a better place and help people win over unnecessary suffering. I truly believe that if you take this book, this conversation to heart, you can use it to transcend to higher consciousness and elevate yourself to a higher existence. Doing so will positively transform how you think and live, and this naturally allows success to be a byproduct of the positive changes in every area of your life.

This blueprint is a way for you to transform and ascend into a NEXT GENERATION HOLISTIC LEADER and WORLD CHANGER. May the transformation begin.

"Everybody has calling.

And your real job in life is to figure out as soon as

possible what that is,

who you were meant to be, and to begin to honor that

in the best way possible for yourself."

-Oprah Winfrey-

INTRODUCTION

Who are you? Why are you here? What is your purpose? How can you use your gifts to live out your purpose and to help others? How can you end your own personal suffering? What would it be like if you lived a beautiful and awe-inspiring life? What does happiness and fulfillment look like to you? What do you want your legacy to be after you leave this earth?

The answers to these questions are essentially the keys to unlock your destiny and your power. Your destiny is connected to everything else on this planet and in the Universe because you are important to the evolution of humankind. You are a force and your existence matters.

However, don't worry if you don't have the answers to any of these questions, yet. The information that awaits you on the proceeding pages will take you from uncertainty to clarity. As you continue reading, I will introduce you to what I believe are key strategies and methods which will help you find and begin walking on the enlightened path to living your best and most successful life by operating at a higher existence.

I've also interlaced some high and low points along my own journey to further illustrate how learning and using specific universal principles and techniques have allowed me to transcend circumstances and low energy vibrations to successfully transform myself and my life. I am currently living and sustaining a higher-level existence, which is key. I hope that by sharing more about myself, my past, and my path that it will help to illuminate and offer insight on your Divine path and help you confidently move toward your best and higher Self.

However, before I do that, I want to make one point very clear. This book is not about me. It's not about my personal experiences, professional challenges, endless uphill battles, triumphs, successes, or many failures. It's about YOU. It's about us. It's about my desire to take the little-known secrets that are shared in the form of high-level inaccessible strategies between the highly successful and make them accessible to everyone, not just a chosen few.

It's my belief that everyone deserves to live a life of beauty, happiness, and fulfillment. We aren't here to merely suffer, endure, and die. You and I are here to enjoy all that life has to offer in abundance. However, in order to do so you need to go beyond a low-level or average existence and access your own higher existence. I have learned through my lived experiences, universal truths and ways of being that are the fundamental elements to consistently living at a higher existence. By doing so, you can obtain and sustain success in every area of your life.

These truths have helped me achieve self-mastery, unwavering self-confidence, material and career success, and status. They've also given me access to the best life has to offer in the form of traveling the world and the ability to achieve things that otherwise would have been inaccessible to me.

However, instead of me only focusing on highlights

and results, I will actually offer these learned truths in simple and digestible ways you can understand and begin using TODAY to change your life for the better. Implementing these truths will allow you to pivot from where you are now toward the direction of the life you're meant to live. It's important that I share the actual process and implementation and not just a list of principles or theories. To me, the latter is ineffective. You need practical steps and illustrations on how to apply each truth to your life, for your benefit. Otherwise, the benefits will remain elusive for you, like they were for me at the beginning of my own journey.

If you're anything like me, you believe you were put on this earth for a reason and you also desire for your life to be meaningful. You might want to attain career success, material wealth, happiness, peace of mind, or simply want to live an enjoyable life with the people you love.

However, if you're also like me, you realized getting the job, the title, the money, and everything else that "they" attribute to success hasn't been enough. You, like me, know there's more to it than just accumulating "stuff" and you are in pursuit of figuring out what "it" is. Wonderful!

One of my life purposes is to motivate, inspire, and lead people to self-actualization. I wrote *The Enlightened Path to Success & Fulfillment* to connect with you and other *lightworkers* in my own quest to do my part in helping to reduce the collective suffering. To ensure that together we can live lives of fulfillment, soul evolution, and accomplishment. It takes all of us, cooperatively, doing our part to impact the world positively.

I'm in eternal gratitude and thanks for the opportunity to share of myself and my learning for the betterment of you and others. More than that, I'm thankful for the time I have with you now to help you deepen your connection with yourself, your gifts, and to empower you to carry the torch forward and help to illuminate the path for others. This book will be a journey. However, I will guide you every step of the way, showing you how all the dots connect, from

Spirituality, Psychology, Human Dynamics, to Business Mechanics, and more.

Let's get started.

THE ENLIGHTENED PATH
PHILOSOPHY

The enlightened path to success and fulfillment begins when a person first comes into awareness of any misalignment within themselves, their environments, their relationships, etc. and seek to correct it. This person begins to realize they have full control over their destiny. Through that insight, they develop a sense of humility and the desire to begin their journey to self-understanding and ultimately to self-mastery.

Complete fulfillment during their lifetime, making a positive impact on humanity, and using the gift(s) they were born with and have developed throughout their life are also a part of the enlightened path to success philosophy. The enlightened path is completed by fully understanding the various dynamics of our world and how everything is interconnected.

It doesn't matter what your vocation is. You can be a musician, a student, barista, fashion designer, factory worker, janitor, teacher, banker, a CFO or CEO. If what you do, you do with the intent to create joy and improve other people's lives, you're already taking enlightened action and are on your path toward success and fulfillment.

There are several key elements I believe it takes to complete the journey to enlightened success. These include:

- Understanding and assessing where you are today and who you are as a person.

- Taking this self-understanding a step further to achieve self-mastery.

- Getting clear about your true purpose and walking in it.

- Understanding others and seeking harmony and alignment in your relationships.

- Understanding core business skills to help you succeed in your professional endeavors.

- Understanding the bigger universal picture and where you fit.

Throughout my life journey, having lived and worked in many countries across the globe, I came to understand the many principles that helped me accelerate in my career and realign with my true Self. From there I've been able to experience fulfillment and happiness in every area of my life.

Along the way, I've learned not to fear anything because everything that I do and have gone through was divinely guided. Our challenges always serve a higher purpose. They occur so that we can learn and grow from them. By facing our challenges straight on, we're equipped and better prepared for the greater to come.

Everything works out for the good. When you don't understand this principle you cause yourself to suffer. Unfortunately, there are millions of people suffering. Many people are ending their lives too soon. That's why it's so important for each of us to develop into the people we need to be so that we can provide unique solutions to help others.

Deep within you, you already have this knowledge and understanding. However, sometimes it's good to be reminded of things so that we can tap back into what we know and need. It's important that you find joy and alignment so that you can experience success and fulfillment.

Once you're in alignment with your purpose and understand yourself better, you'll be free to share your knowledge and skills with others. Your joy will be multiplied. That's what it will take to make this world a better place, to reduce the collective suffering, and enter into collective fulfillment and collective soul evolution.

What makes my philosophy different from others is that it moves past the concept of 'just' the material consciousness. Abundance includes money, but also love, health, harmonious interpersonal relationships, peace of mind, etc.

The human mind over the years, decades, and centuries has been remolded to be primarily individualistic and profit-oriented. It's true that you as an individual need to walk your own path to personal achievement, success, and abundance in all aspects of life. However, it should be done with an enlightened viewpoint of caring about your impact on others, the free exchange of information, and understanding interconnectedness, so that you transform into a more holistic human being and can then teach and show others how to do the same.

The *Law of Compensation*, which I will touch on later in the book, states that one gets compensated at the level of their contribution to humanity. So, once your contribution to humanity grows, the energy of money will flourish naturally in your life.

The core of my philosophy deals with transcending individualistic consciousness and ultimately realizing the fact that we are connected to one another and to be able to see the bigger picture in that.

As we each journey on our respective enlightened paths, we will influence others to do the same and continue the positive cycle forward. Living out our purpose helps others realize theirs and come into alignment. Collective alignment is the key to changing the trajectory of suffering. Each individual person is responsible for walking their own path. By becoming fulfilled and successful, they can ignite the flame of the people they influence. This is the win-win.

We all need one another. We may have different personalities, backgrounds, desires, and purposes, but at the core we are all the same. The enlightened path to success and fulfillment is a journey each of us must take to be who we're truly meant to be for our sake and the sake of every other soul on this planet. This philosophy is our blueprint to getting there. We will use mindfulness, focused intention, and meditation to aid us on the journey. They will help us stay clear and present as we move forward.

MEDITATION & WHY IT'S CRITICAL

Meditation is a practice where an individual uses a technique – such as mindfulness, or focusing the mind on a particular object, thought, or activity – to train attention and awareness, and to achieve a mentally clear and emotionally calm state of being. Meditation is a habitual process of training your mind to be quiet and emptying out your endless thoughts.

You can use it to increase awareness of yourself and your surroundings. Many people us mediation to reduce stress and develop better concentration skills.

A meditation practice is also used to develop other beneficial habits and feelings, such as a positive mood and outlook, self-discipline, healthy sleep patterns, and even increased pain tolerance. Other benefits of having a meditation practice include:

- Anxiety relief and management

- Promoting emotional health

- Enhanced self-awareness

- Lengthening your attention span

There are two major styles of meditation, focused-attention mediation, and open-monitoring meditation.

Focused-attention meditation directs attention on a single object, thought, sound or visualization. It emphasizes ridding your mind of attention and distraction. Meditation may focus on breathing, a mantra, or a calming sound.

Open-monitoring meditation improves broadened awareness of all aspects of your environment, train of thought, and sense of Self. It may include becoming aware of thoughts, feelings, or impulses you might normally try to suppress.

"Whenever you step out of the noise of thinking, that is meditation, and a different state of consciousness arises." Eckhart Tolle

I was first introduced to meditation at 29. In 2013 I went to a Buddhist temple while in Kuala Lumpur, Malaysia. A monk at the temple saw me sitting down alone and invited to teach me a walking meditation. From there, I followed guided meditations online until I eventually developed my own style and practice.

I can honestly tell you that without my daily meditation practice, I'm convinced I would have long-since developed some physical or mental health issue or perhaps become reliant on controlled substances. I'm not sure I would have been able to cope with the enormous amount of pressure and the toll that a demanding work environment and life in general have on your mental, physical, and emotional state, day in and day out.

As you'll discover as you continue reading, I have made most of my journey solo. I didn't have any family close by or people that I trusted early on that I could talk to. The challenging trials, doubts and fears, and being so isolated all the time, took its toll on my body and mind. I felt myself noticing the dangers that could arise if I didn't figure out a way to handle and process my emotions, fears, and mounting stress in a healthy and constructive way.

You might have heard the phrase, "when the student is ready, the teacher appears." It was my higher Self that led me to that Buddhist temple on that particular day, knowing that I needed help and a way to deal with the all the heavy things in life without destroying myself and sacrificing my destiny in the process.

Personally, meditation helps me calm my mind and regulate my body and emotions. During meditation, I'm also able to enter into a space where I receive supernatural guidance and heightened intuitive direction for myself or advice for others (known as channeling).

Daily meditation allows me to clear out my emotions and alleviate all my stress. I don't give stress the opportunity to sit and fester, causing dis-ease in my mind, body, or emotions. Meditation allows me to flush it out completely so that I can start each day fresh and clear about my intentions and the things I want to attract.

Most days when I wake up, I first show gratitude for

the gift of life. Then I take about 25 to 35 minutes to meditate, followed by going to the gym, and listening to an inspirational video or audiobook. In the evening before going to bed, I put on my special meditation playlist and get into a deep meditation.

I don't have a strict regimen because my meditation needs vary based on what I have going on in my life. I stay in tune to what I feel I need to do daily. Sometimes, I may stop an activity to do a quick meditation and re-center myself or my body moves a certain way, and that movement indicates the need to meditate and get realigned.

Meditation is not limited to any religion or spiritual practice either. Anyone can meditate no matter what religious tradition they associate with.

Starting in the next section, you will begin working with different meditations that I incorporated throughout the book to prepare you to receive and integrate the information that I will be sharing. We will use the focused-attention meditation practice here.

As you develop your own practice, I believe you'll

find meditation beneficial on your journey. You can do it for as little as a minute at any time of the day to help you center yourself and develop more self-awareness. Once you learn the basics of meditation, you will realize how simple it is to focus on the present moment.

Worry, busyness, and stress can cause our minds to take us on some crazy rides. It can remind us of a difficult past or have us worry about millions of unlikely future scenarios. This creates unnecessary suffering. Too much thinking about the past causes depression while too much thinking about the future creates anxiety.

However, anytime you begin to feel overwhelmed with what's going on in your life, use your meditation practice to go within and re-align yourself. Staying present is the best way to stay focused on the outcomes you can control and that is key to making successful outcomes a habit.

MAKING SPACE MEDITATION

B efore we go any further, it's necessary to take a moment to prepare you to receive new knowledge. I have included the below mediation to help you make space for what you actually want to manifest in your life. Meaning, you need to clear out what no longer serves you so you're ready to receive what will aid you in your enlightened quest for success. With this meditation, I want to help you fully release what might be holding you back and prime you for the new that lies ahead.

I know that every person reading this book will probably be in a different place in life. For some people, self-awareness and tuning-inward might be the norm, and for others it might be a foreign concept altogether. For that reason, I want to point out that it's natural to feel resistance to change and to fresh ways of thinking, even if they are what's best for you. That's why I'm pausing here and taking a moment to guide you through what might be your hundredth or very first meditation.

The intention behind this meditation is to help you connect with yourself on a deeper level and for you to clear any potential mental blocks or adverse feelings you have about opening yourself up to alternative possibilities and the new knowledge waiting for you.

I realize that it's impossible to close your eyes and read at the same time. A better way to approach this meditation if you're reading a physical book or eBook is to record yourself reading the meditation out loud on your phone or another electronic device and play it back when you're ready so you can repeat each affirmation as you go through the meditation. Let's begin.

I invite you to close your eyes now. Take three slow, deep breaths. Breathing in through your nose and out through your mouth on each exhale. It might feel good to make an audible sighing sound on the exhale.

I invite you to repeat the following affirmations out loud.

- I deserve to be happy and fulfilled.

- I welcome new knowledge and new possibilities.

- I am willing to learn.

- I am willing to upgrade my life.

- I welcome all new guidance meant for my highest good as I journey ahead.

- I open my mind & receive good into my life.

- I welcome good into my body and my soul.

- I'm allowing myself to transcend my previous state of consciousness.

- I am in line with my true calling and my inner fulfillment.

- I am safe. Everything is and will be okay.

- I'm open to receiving inner peace, inner harmony, and inner balance.

- I am deserving and worthy of all this now.

Take another deep breath and picture yourself opening up to all these new possibilities. What does your new reality look like? How do you look in your picture? Are you smiling? Do you feel lighter? More capable? Joyful? Are you excited about what's coming? Welcome it!

Now take another deep breath in and visualize a beautiful glowing energy surrounding you and protecting you, welcoming you into this next chapter of your life. Take a moment to send gratitude and love out into this energy. Take one final deep breath and on the exhale whisper, "thank you," and open your eyes.

Welcome back! Your new world is awaiting you!

Take a moment to readjust to being in your body and in the present moment. You can do this clearing meditation as many times as needed for you to feel you're ready to journey forward. Sometimes one time will not be enough. It's important to me that you get everything you need to transform your life for the better and experience lasting change. This is not just a feel-good type of book. It's a life manual, meant to challenge you and help you achieve the life you truly desire for yourself. Let's continue.

MY EARLY YEARS

As far back as I can remember I sensed something different about myself that had nothing to do with my origins or my being bi-racial. I could always sense and feel an energy that allowed me to see beyond what I could see with my eyes.

I was born in Libreville, Gabon, on the west coast of Africa. My mom, Chantal was 17 at the time and my dad was a Vietnamese businessman in his forties. He was a very wealthy man who showed kindness and interest in my mother. A relationship developed between them and they fell in love.

However, their romance was short-lived once my mom discovered he was already married to another woman and had two daughters. From that point on, they separated. Shortly after I was born, my mom got sick and my grandmother stepped in to raise me. I don't recall having any interaction with my father as a child. I am not sure if he ever hugged me or showed any interest in my life.

Growing up half African and half Vietnamese caused me to stand out. No one else was mixed in my family. However, I wasn't treated better or worse because of this. My grandmother treated me like I was her own child. We had a very special connection. In the summers I went with her to a nearby island for vacation. There's one summer in particular that sticks out to me and reminds me of the evidence of a Divine presence working in my life even at a young age.

I had to be around five years old at the time. I remember playing in the water with my extended family, aunts, and uncles, who were young teenagers then. Everyone took turns playing with me and monitoring me, until suddenly everyone heard my grandmother yell that lunch was ready. Everyone sprinted out of the water and toward the house. They forgot me.

A wave came in before I could make my way onto the sand and carried me further from shore. I remember my body tensing in fear. The rip current pulled me so far out that our house kept getting smaller and smaller in the distance. I was still so small; I didn't know how to swim yet.

I remember a flash of panic inside because instinctively I knew something was wrong. I was there in the water all alone and drifting further away from safety with every passing moment. I sensed danger, even though I'd never experienced it before.

Surely, this should have been the end of my story. Then I heard a voice inside me speak.

"Calm down." the voice said. "Sink down to the bottom of the water."

At five years old, I doubt if I could rationalize like that of my adult Self. When you're a child, you do what you're told, usually without question. You're more trusting of everyone and everything.

I remember beginning to sink and going down deeper in the water until I got to the bottom.

"Stretch out flat. Spread your arms and legs out

wide. Cling to the floor and walk back."

I dug my little hands into the sand and pushed myself forward with my feet. I started crawling under the water.

"Everything will be fine. Trust me," the voice reassured me.

I have no idea how I held my breath or how long it took, but I made it back to shore and dry ground. By then, my family was outside looking for me. I remember the look of amazement and shock on everyone's face as my eyes searched the crowd for the comfort of my grandmother's presence.

By a sheer miracle, I survived and was perfectly fine. I have many more stories of experiencing evidence of the miraculous happening in my life. Evidence of Divine protection and guidance allowing me to overcome temporary challenges has shown up to rescue me repeatedly. Confirming to me that there is a higher power always concerned about me and ready to help me in my time of need.

Needless to say, everyone was much more careful

with me from then on to ensure my safety.

The years I spent with my grandmother were priceless and the bond that we built was beyond special. A couple of years passed, my mother got well and then decided to move to France in order to try to make a better life for herself and eventually me. I was seven. She sat me down one evening after dinner and explained,

"Kevin, I'm leaving to go to France. Once I get settled there, I'll send for you to come and live with me. Who do you want to stay with now?" she asked me.

My choice consisted of two uncles and their families. I remember my seven year old rationale at the time. I chose one over the other simply off the fact that I knew one uncle wouldn't hit me if I peed in my bed, and the other one would punish me if he caught me peeing in my bed.

My answer was simple, "I want to go to my uncle Henri."

A week after our conversation, my mom left for France and I went to live with my uncle Henri, his wife,

Mamie, their two daughters, and another cousin they were taking care of. My uncle was a flight attendant, and at that time we considered it a top job in Gabon. My aunt was a secretary, which was also a great job back in the day. We were seen as wealthy or well-off in the eyes of the community. We lived in a good house, in a decent neighborhood, and I attended a good school. From a material standpoint, I never missed anything. It was a loving environment. My aunt and uncle were very kind to me, and I know they loved me as their own child.

However, even though they were family, it wasn't the same as me being with my mom, nor did it make up for the absence of my father. I remember feeling a deep sense of abandonment and sadness. Since my father was never in my life, when my mom left me behind, I just felt really lonely inside. I remember crying all the time, thinking about my mom. It took her two years before she could save enough money to send for me to come to France to be with her. Those two years were long and worrisome for me.

The six of us lived together as a makeshift family until one day my mom called out of the blue and told my aunt that she was ready for me to come be with her in France.

It was a Friday. I still remember. My aunt walked toward me with tears in her eyes, but also smiling.

"Kevin, your mom called. She said she bought your ticket, and she's ready. She's asking for you." Her voice strained with sadness. "She says you can fly there tomorrow or you can wait until Monday for your uncle to come back from his trip so you can say a proper goodbye."

"No!" I yelled with excitement. "I want to go tomorrow."

I didn't know it then, but it was probably very sad for everyone because I left so suddenly. I wasn't able to say a proper goodbye to my uncle or other family. But I was missing my mom so much and so desperately that I just wanted to go and find her.

The next day, I flew alone to Paris, France. I had one of those plastic, see-through holders around my neck with my papers and ticket that they give to minors flying alone. I had another distant uncle who was also a flight attendant who took care of me on the plane. He brought me to business class for a moment, and then he brought me to see the pilots and the view from the cockpit.

I remember how amazing it all was and how excited I felt at such an adventure.

I arrived in Paris the next day. My mom was standing nervously at the gate with her boyfriend at the time waiting for me to deplane. Seeing her again after over two years was a dream come true. A liberation. I was also in shock. I couldn't believe it. I cried heavily and was so proud and relieved to know that she did not in fact abandon me for good.

After an emotional and joyful reunion, we drove from Paris down to the south-western city of Marmande, France. The drive seemed like it would never end, but it was only about eight hours. I later learned that the area is known as 'tomato country' in France.

Although I was still euphoric with the excitement of being reunited with my mom, my first plane ride experience, and the new environment, I noticed the stark contrast between the lifestyle I had been living with my aunt and uncle and that of my mom in France.

Before I arrived, she lived in a small studio apartment with her little dog, Fifille, next to a hospital. Now, it was me, her, and Fifille. It was clear that we didn't have money. From a material standpoint we were poor. It didn't bother me at first because even though I had everything provided for me by my aunt and uncle, there was still a huge void in my life without the presence of my mother. Even though my mom didn't have much, she gave me a lot of love. Just being with her and being close to her was enough for me.

Growing up in Marmande, France, I knew from society's standpoint, being a poor kid, living with a single mom, getting government support in order to eat and have a place to live, we were at the bottom. I often felt like I was missing so much, but I knew my mom was doing her best and I didn't want to ask her for more.

However, when I started school not having what I needed became a challenge because I was thrown into the world of comparison. I had to wait for my mom to receive government aid before I could get new clothes or shoes. My friends at school had everything. The latest brand name clothes, good shoes, nice toys. They also had something else that I was missing, but that wasn't as obvious. They had two parents.

Their moms and dads picked them up in nice cars after school. Me on the other hand, I walked home, often alone, after school. The walk took me between 20 to 30 minutes every day. When I first started school, my mom walked with me, but after I knew the route, it was just me on my own. I was around nine.

During holiday vacations, my friends went to visit their families in larger cities or spent their holidays in the mountains or at the beach. I spent my holiday vacations at home, in our small studio apartment, next to the hospital. I had myself and Fifille for entertainment, while my mom worked.

In my pre-teen years, I struggled heavily with self-identity and self-esteem issues. Often feeling sad and out of place. I had to accept that there was nothing I could do about missing out on the latest material things or not having a proper family structure like my friends did. I can remember times when I didn't know how to cope with my gripping feelings of sadness, anger, and frustration during those years. As a result, I mostly tried to ignore them.

I wanted to know, "Why couldn't I be like my friends? Why wasn't I happy? Why didn't I have what they had? Why did my mom have to struggle so hard to provide for us when others were living easier lives?" Sometimes I got angry with my mom because I wondered why she didn't have the things we needed. It wasn't fair that she didn't have a better job. A fancy car. A nicer place to live. We deserved those things too.

Deserving or not, we didn't have them and there was nothing I could do in that moment to change our reality. Deep inside I knew it wasn't my mom's fault, so I stopped focusing on blaming my mom and other people and accepted it for what it was. I also felt that our situation was only temporary and that one day everything would somehow change. It had to.

One thing I was grateful for was that my mom was very kind and very strong. She never showed me that she was desperate and hopeless. To this day, that is something I commend her for. She always tried to make things seem as if everything was fine. She always kept a smile on her face and didn't want to burden me with any sadness or despair. I admire her for that.

Time passed quickly. I stayed in Marmande, France with my mom. I grew up.

What I couldn't have known then were the lingering effects that the suppressed feelings of abandonment, anger, frustration, resentment, and living in lack had on me as a young child and would continue to have on me as I grew up. At the time, I didn't know that ignoring my feelings and emotions wasn't the same as making them go away. These issues showed up time and time again, causing me to suffer, and I couldn't figure out why.

Acceptance, forgiveness, and surrender would be needed before any lasting change could take place. It took me time to figure this out.

I kept hitting walls. The pain kept building on itself.

Until I did.

"It's unnatural for our lives to be hopelessly encumbered. Endowed with the potential to re-envision and reform, we generate our own path."
-Kuan Yin-

BOOK ONE:

UNDERSTANDING YOURSELF

"It matters not how strait the gate,

how charged with punishments the scroll,

I am the master of my fate; I am the captain of my

soul."

-William Ernest Henley-

UNDERSTANDING YOURSELF

There were a few things that I knew about myself innately even as a young child. However, learned behaviors and unfortunate situations often overshadow what we know about ourselves. They distract us as we try to improve our circumstances and get a good footing in life overall. Who we become and who we are at our core many times conflict with each other, further complicating our lives.

Early in my journey, I went with the flow a lot. I believed things just happened to you. I believed that everyone was subject to a certain fate, and that this fate was already determined when you're born. I figured perhaps with a little luck I would get a decent job and just maybe I'd end up having a decent life. It wasn't until I started tuning inward and sensing that this mentality didn't line up with who I truly was at my core that I questioned these very primitive beliefs.

What I discovered on the other side was the real me. I discovered who I was and who I wanted to be. I also realized that the perspective I held around my limitations was just a reflection of the environment I

grew up in. It wasn't actually me, and it wasn't my fate to remain stuck and misaligned to who I truly was.

Understanding who you are, what motivates you, where you are in life, and what you really want are all critical in helping you figure out how to change and transform into the best and higher version of yourself. Before you can attain and sustain any real level of success, wealth, or status in life you have to elevate your consciousness and become the person able to handle what you desire.

You can only attract to you who you are. You are energy. You vibrate at a certain frequency based on the thoughts and actions you focus on day-to-day. However, introspection is not something that our hyper-busy society touts as being beneficial to your health and well-being, but it is. Only by going within and learning about who you are at your core, can you figure out the causes of your repeated patterns, behaviors, beliefs, and experiences and then do something about them. Treating symptoms won't provide the cure for what really ails you.

A keen sense of self-awareness, humility, and gratitude is essential for you to discover your specific enlightened path to success and fulfillment. Being self-aware allows you to harness your strengths and develop and build on areas of weakness. It will also help you to improve your self-control and any negative behaviors because you'll be able to be less reactive to the circumstances that are beyond your control. Once you know who you are, you can release victimhood mentality and behavior and take a more proactive approach to living life. The first step is discovering how your mind works. Your mind holds the answers you seek and the results you want to see.

YOUR CONSCIOUS & SUBCONSCIOUS MIND: THE FUNDAMENTALS

The first concept around understanding yourself better is getting to know your mind. Your mind consists of two parts, your conscious and subconscious. The conscious part of your mind is aware of what you see and are doing right now. You may be watching TV, or looking at your friend standing across the room, or sitting on your couch scrolling through your Instagram feed. Your conscious mind is processing these things in the present moment.

The subconscious part of your mind is like a master recording machine of experiences and beliefs. It's the part of the mind that perceives beyond what you see and records everything from the moment you were conceived all the way to where you are today.

We associate the conscious mind with what we see, feel, and understand in this moment. The subconscious mind records and stores the knowledge we take in and forms our beliefs and our behaviors based on what we went through over our lifetime. It's the equivalent of a black box in a plane.

Why is this important? It's important to understand how the mind works because a lot of what we do we're not conscious of. We go throughout our lives on autopilot with our subconscious mind controlling us.

Have you ever stopped to think about how you open the door before doing it? Probably not, you just do it. You don't have to think about how to operate your car beforehand in order to drive to work. You learned how to drive through instruction and practice, and since then, it's instinctive.

Opening a door, driving a car, cooking, riding a bicycle, or swimming, these are activities that if you know how to do them, the process was automatically recorded and stored so that you don't have to think about it consciously again. You just do them and move on to the next thing.

You might be wondering, "why is this a bad thing?" Well, with the basic examples I just illustrated, it's not.

Being able to do simple everyday tasks without needing to spend time and energy thinking about them first is beneficial. In this way, the subconscious mind is serving you well.

However, what about when your stored memory distorts the way you perceive reality today because the information that's stored is no longer valid? Your subconscious mind doesn't know that times have changed and that the dangerous situation you encountered at six years old has no impact on what you perceive as being your reality today.

What's tricky is that just like any other machine, the subconscious mind doesn't question or have the faculty to reason. It takes your input and experiences, stores them, and makes them available to you when you need them. Over time, your recorded information became your beliefs. Your beliefs became your behaviors and your behaviors became your actions. Repeated action is what drives your results in life and dictates your quality of life either positively or negatively.

Subconscious Mind:
From Experience to Results chart

An example of a negative behavior based on recorded beliefs would be the fact that many people struggle financially. Debt often causes financial ruin in people's lives. Simply put, debt results from spending more than you earn. It doesn't matter why people go into debt. Each individual has specific behaviors. However, if looked at closely, spending more than you earn has to do with your relationship with money.

You formed your relationship with money from the childhood beliefs you were taught about money.

Many people feel they don't make enough money. They work for the same income for years. They don't save. They view their relationship with money as a struggle so they view money through the lens of lack. This is easily illustrated by the language they use when they talk about money.

- Life is tough.

- Money is hard to attain.

- There aren't any good jobs.

- I don't have the education to earn more.

- Things are too expensive.

- I'll never earn enough to live well.

Perception is everything. Could these things be accurate? Absolutely. However, what's most likely at play here is that these are the recordings this person heard as a child from their parents and they're simply living out their recorded beliefs in their finances as adults.

Every person shapes their own lived reality based on what they believe about themselves, their environment, the people around them, etc. Our subconscious mind recorded information from different sources, some of the most impactful information was recorded from people of authority during our childhood (both positive or negative). Then during adulthood our repeated experiences get deeply rooted into the subconscious mind further strengthening those earlier beliefs.

A lot of the things we believe originated in our childhood without us knowing how it would affect our lives. The first step to transform your outdated beliefs and actions is to figure out what you believe and why.

In the next chapter, you'll take some time retracing your steps and getting to the source of your current mindset.

DIVING INTO YOUR SUBCONSCIOUS
MIND: TAKING INVENTORY

L et's go back in time. In this exercise we'll focus on your beliefs around money. However, you can follow the same process if your issues deal with other things like self-esteem, relationships, self-confidence, etc. You can apply this exercise to any area of your life where you hold negative beliefs that create challenges in your life.

It's important to remember that any challenge you are facing today has a seed of opportunity hidden within it. First you need to find out where it all started. Once you know the root issue, you can work to change what your subconscious mind has been playing negatively in the background.

Step One:

Grab a notebook and a pen. It'll be more beneficial for you to write out your memories regarding money.

- What did you hear from your parents, the people

in your community, and people in authority when you were a child regarding money?

- What did you see? How did you feel about money?

- What were your early experiences with money?

- What are five statements you heard most about money?

From birth to about 14, your subconscious is very sensitive to learning and programming. Think about your life, your childhood, and the language that was used to describe money and your thoughts and feelings around money as you grew up and as an adult.

Step Two:

Write the first five statements that come to mind. You can always go back and add more. If you were brought up in an environment where money was scarce, you might have heard your parents say, "There isn't enough money. Money doesn't grow on trees." What do you think now? What about the tried-and-true anthems, "Money can't make you happy," or "you need to work hard for money?"

As you grew up and heard these types of beliefs repeated over and over, coming from people you loved and trusted, you naturally believed them. Their complaining and suffering with relation to money was recorded in your subconscious mind and is playing back these broken records in your reality today.

Step Three:

If the five statements you heard most about money were negative, I want you to write a positive statement that cancels out each negative statement or belief on a brand new clean page. The original page should only have the negative statements. The fresh page should list the positive statements you created specifically to cancel out your identified negative beliefs.

A few positive examples are, "Money is a beautiful energy available for the achievement of my dreams. Money flows to me naturally. Being wealthy is a wonderful thing, it allows me to help others." You must be very specific when writing out your new positive beliefs. The positive statements need to relate specifically to the negative things you heard growing up. They cannot just be general statements.

Deep down, now you might believe something else entirely and desire to have a different relationship with money altogether. However, your subconscious mind is a neutral party. It doesn't distinguish between the past or present. It simply recalls what you've been told or what you've experienced over and over through repetition as your truth.

Naturally, if you've recorded a lot of negative beliefs about money from early childhood into adolescence, those beliefs became stronger. Without realizing it, you've gone through life making choices and decisions based on this negative programming.

Guess what the outcome is? A reality of never having enough money.

As I mentioned before, this inventory exercise can also be used to identify negative beliefs regarding your relationships.

Again, go back in time and observe yourself as a child growing up. What type of relationships did you see around you? How was the relationship between your mother and father? What was your first experience with a man or a woman like? Was it positive? Negative? Listen with your inner child's ears to the language that was used to describe the adult relationships that you grew up around.

As you listen to your memories, which your subconscious mind is playing back for you as you access these memories, you'll be able to correlate what you experienced as a child to your lived reality today. This is the power of the subconscious mind.

Repeat the above exercise for each area of your life that you need to rewire from negative to positive. Do your best to release any negative emotions associated with each statement as you rewrite it into a positive one. You don't need to hold on to that baggage anymore. You need to be light and fluid so that in the next chapters you can act on the knowledge you discover and really begin to pivot from where you are to where you really desire to be.

Once you've taken the negative statements and

turned them into positive ones, I want you to take the page(s) with the old negative statements and beliefs and burn them. Assure your safety and the safety of others by doing this outside and away from children or animals.

Maybe everything you heard as a child about money, relationships, and life in general wasn't all negative. Great! On the flip side, all the good things we've witnessed, heard, and experienced growing up laid a positive foundation that encouraged us to have more positive experiences and outcomes in our adult lives.

Either way, our early experiences shaped who we are today. If you were told you could do and achieve great things, if you lived in an environment where you saw your parents happy and the relationship was based on trust, respect, and mutual love, then you've probably had success at recreating those experiences in your own life.

There are exceptions to every generalization. However, the rule of thumb is positive creates more positive and negative creates more negative.

The good news about the subconscious mind is that there is a way for us to change the beliefs we're no longer in agreement with, which I will expand on further in the next section.

However, now that you've looked honestly at your life today and have identified the areas you struggle in the most, you've taken the first and most important step to working on rewiring those negative beliefs into more positive ones.

Spend as much time as needed fully completing this exercise for each area of your life you seek to transform. I don't recommend you move on until you spend sufficient time strolling back down memory lane. This will help you be more objective in the next section where we'll explore your lived reality now. Doing this exercise will also help you connect the dots and see how you ended up where you are.

Know that you are not your past. You're better. Now let's work on changing your subconscious mind to match who you want to be today and in the future.

"Surrendering the old you, creates space for the new, allowing for your life to unfold in alignment with the highest order."

-Anonymous-

REWIRE YOUR SUBCONSCIOUS MIND

(Using My RSM Technique)

I created this technique to completely rewire the limiting, subconscious beliefs I unknowingly developed as a child and therefore unconsciously reproduced as an adult around money, deserving love, self-confidence (am I good enough), my self-worth (do I deserve it), and doubting my existence (why am I even here?). This technique combines self-hypnosis, Neuro Linguistic Programming (NLP), visualization, and autosuggestion.

My RSM (Rewire Subconscious Mind) method took me years to understand and develop. However, with time, patience, and intent, I put the pieces of the puzzle together and connected the dots. I was also already fully committed to my own personal development, the process of self-mastery, and I was also eager to experience lasting change after seeing it work for so many others.

I was living in Los Angeles at the time, near Culver

City Studios, in a small studio apartment. I had consciously decided to live with only the basics, a bed, a fridge, and nothing else. I can remember a day when I was lying on my bed, feeling really pissed off at God. I was so desperate then. I felt lost as to why I wasn't able to get to a place where I could just be happy.

While work was going well, I was struggling with my self-confidence, finances, and experiencing a lack of good relationships. There was always something "off." I had already invested a sizable amount of money in "self-help" books, seminars, etc., and had spent a lot of time researching techniques and strategies that were supposed to positively impact my life. But I wasn't experiencing any lasting change.

I knew in my gut that the "secrets" worked, but felt stuck. I was knowledge heavy with no insight on how to apply all the knowledge and connect it together. The burning question was, "how could I implement what I was learning into my life so that it was relevant and actually life changing for me in the way it was for others."

I remember crying out to God in pure anguish and frustration:

"If we're made from you, if it's true that you gave us the pen to write the life we desire and enjoy this life journey, how fair is it that we have to spend so much money on seminars, books, therapists, motivational speakers, and coaches, but we can never get to a place where we figure it out and really master our own faith?"

As I finished my intense inquiry, I remember my eyes roaming back and forth over the walls of my apartment where I use to pin up handwritten notes and quotes on topics dealing with the mind, universal laws, NLP, etc. I literally covered my four walls with information, but the knowledge alone wasn't giving me the tools to manifest the results in my life.

I was so upset and filled with utter hopelessness that I don't even remember falling asleep. I just remember waking up and feeling an enormous sense of calm within. An apparent peace replaced the anger and helplessness that had lulled me to sleep.

Sunshine warmed my face, surrounding me with an illuminating light. The sound of birds singing outside was the only sound until a voice deep inside of me replied to my earlier questioning,

"I hear you, Son. Now I will allow you to put all this knowledge together and connect the dots. You will develop a proven technique for not only your life, but that you will share with the world. Too many of my creations are ending their lives too soon because of stress, disease, accidents, and despair from not knowing who they are or why they exist."

From that point forward, everything became clear. The dots suddenly connected. I could see which techniques I needed to use in order to properly integrate the knowledge I had into my life in a way that would change it for the better. I was also able to easily repeat and master each technique and eventually begin sharing them with others once I experienced positive results myself.

I believe we have the ability to rewire ourselves up to 95%. For the remaining 5%, I recommend working with an excellent Hypnotherapist (Ericksonian trained) who can help you wrap the remainder up in only three sessions.

Now it's time for you to put my method to work and see how YOU can use it to begin rewiring yourself and your unwanted beliefs.

Just like with our earlier meditation, I encourage you to record the instructions to this exercise on your phone or another electronic device before attempting it so that you're able to guide yourself through it properly without needing to read through it over and over, which can serve as a distraction to getting into the deep state of relaxation needed to achieve hypnosis.

Before recording it, read through all seven steps at least once before beginning, just so you're aware of what you'll be doing and can be more relaxed and comfortable about knowing what to expect before you begin. You'll also need the positive statements you wrote from the previous exercise handy.

Step One:

Sit somewhere comfortable, quiet, and safe where you won't be interrupted or disturbed. Feel free to put on soothing white noise or soft instrumental music at a low volume level in the background.

I invite you to pick something in front of you, a place on the wall or an object, something neutral, that you can fix your eyes on and can continue to concentrate on without moving.

In my case, I'm looking at the switch on the heater which is at eye level, and easy for me to focus on without my needing to shift my body in any way.

Look at the neutral object you've chosen to focus on. Take three deep breaths. First, inhale through your nose and exhale slowly through your mouth, keeping your eyes open. Take another deep breath in, slowly, and exhale very slowly out through your mouth. On your third breath, inhale, and this time on the slow exhale, close your eyes.

Continue to breathe slowly and stay focused on your breathing.

Step Two:

Now, with your eyes still closed, from your heart, call into your soul, your worshiped God (across all faiths), your angels, spiritual guides, the Universe, or any support based on your beliefs, to come and form a circle of love around you. This circle will protect you as you begin this journey into your Subconscious mind.

Step Three:

With your eyes still closed, imagine there is a beautiful light surrounding you. Feel free to give it a bright, beautiful color. Let's say blue. The light is creating a tunnel around you. A beautiful blue tunnel. This energy is surrounding you and extends up to the sky.

Step Four:

Now imagine there's another beautiful light, a white light that comes out the top of your head and expands slowly. It's a soothing light. A healing light. The white light travels down to your forehead, over the back of your head, to your eyes, nose, throat, and mouth, and it slowly illuminates through you as it travels down your body.

The light moves down to your chest, over your stomach, to your lower back, your pelvis, and thighs, taking its time. See the beautiful light expanding to your knees, your calves, your feet, and finally your entire body.

In this moment, fully illuminated, you should sense your body fully relaxed. Your head is moving dropping slowly toward your chest. Your breathing is slow and peaceful. You're fully illuminated with this beautiful white light, which gives you a deep sense of calmness, peace, security, and complete relaxation.

Step Five:

As you get deeper into this peaceful space, repeat to yourself, "Relax, relax, relax. I am safe." Visualize yourself walking down a flight of beautiful stairs. These stairs can be anywhere. They can be in nature, by the beach, on a mountain top, or surrounded by other sources of beauty.

However, I want you to actually see yourself

standing on the staircase, fully there having the experience. You're at the top of them preparing to walk down. You're going to descend the stairs one step at a time, while counting, starting at 20.

Begin by taking a step, 20, 19, 18, 17, as you continue to go down, keep counting. 16, 15, 14, 13, 12, 11. As you go down, you are gaining access and going deeper and deeper into your inner being. You keep walking down deeper and deeper within. 10, 9, 8, 7, 6, 5, 4, 3, 2, 1, 0. At zero say to yourself, "Deep sleep now."

Step Six:

Continue to breathe slowly. Stay focused on your breathing as you maintain the feeling of calm and peace from the soothing energy surround you. You may feel chills or feel your body shudder. Just continue to breathe for another minute, while you slowly repeat, "Deeper. I'm safe. I'm connected. I'm healing. Calmness and peace."

At this moment, you've entered the realm of your subconscious mind. You should now be in a deep state of meditation or trance. In this space visualize yourself walking towards a beautiful flame. You can give it a beautiful bright color. See yourself walking in front of it. This flame represents your soul, your subconscious mind, and the essence of our Universe, right there in front of you.

In that space, continue to breathe deeply and slowly with peace, then repeat:

- Whatever needs to be healed, be healed.

- Whatever needs to be said, be said.

- Whatever needs to be done, be done.

- Whatever needs to be heard, be heard.

- What needs to be forgiven, be forgiven.

- What needs to be aligned, be aligned.

- Whatever needs to be released, be released.

At this moment, allow your subconscious mind to reveal the answers to these prompts. Next, I invite you to open your eyes slightly and repeat the positive statements you created for yourself in the previous section. Do your best to stay in the present moment.

Keep your focus on your breathing and the visualization of the beautiful flame of light. In this space you have full access to your subconscious mind. Repeat each positive statement you wrote. Repeat your list 15 times. Five times aloud to yourself. Five times as a whisper and five times silently.

As you repeat each positive statement, tap on various parts of your body intuitively to anchor the statement in your physical and conscious mind.

For example, slowly and gently begin tapping with your fist three fingers, on the top of your head, on your forehead, chest, or wherever you're guided. Trust your body to show you where the old anchors of negative beliefs lie and follow its intelligence while repeating your list the full 15 times (5 times aloud, 5 times whispering, 5 times silently).

In that space, also call in the amount of money you wish to manifest. You may say, "I'm earning an income of $_____ or greater every month."

Step Seven:

Once you've repeated your positive statements, it's

now time to express gratitude from your heart for the experience.

Close your eyes again while focusing on your breathing. Inhaling and exhaling slowly, start to count from 0, 1, 2, 3, 4, 5, and say out loud, "wake up now," then snap your fingers once.

Important Notes:

The best time to access your subconscious mind is first thing in the morning and just before going to bed. These are moments where your conscious mind is vulnerable and tired or not fully awakened yet, so it's easier to get through that mental barrier and get access to your master recording machine.

I recommend performing the steps I've just shared for 31 days nonstop, both in the morning and at night with the same list of new positive beliefs. After 31 days, you can dispose of the initial list and create a new one depending on the limitations you still seek to address.

To experience lasting change and alter your subconscious mind, the rewiring exercise and meditation should be done first thing in the morning and right before bed consistently for at least 31 days without missing a session.

MY RSM TECHNIQUE CHART

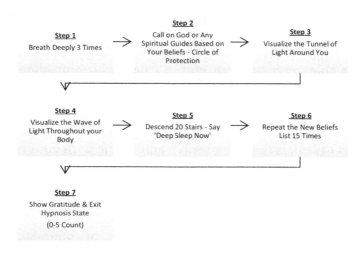

Repetition is critical in order to swap beliefs that are no longer serving you. The old beliefs have been active for so long, the only way to dislodge and replace them is through constant repetition of new beliefs. The process takes 31 days at the very minimum in order to swap out your old beliefs that aren't working and producing good results into new beliefs that will allow you to experience a higher quality of life.

After two or three days, it's likely that you'll start to feel differently. But that feeling won't last if you don't continue the rewiring process consistently for the full 31 days. If you do the exercise for a day or two and feel good but then you decide to stop, you risk allowing the old beliefs to reemerge and you may not be able to see or experience the desired lasting change. Practicing my technique for the full 31 days or longer will reprogram your subconscious mind with your new set of beliefs that are positive and in line with your true Self and current desires.

In the example of money, imagine if now your internal recording plays messages of abundance, positive money relationships, and success. Well, that message will go out into the universe and activate the law of attraction. Without you realizing, suddenly new opportunities will show up and unexpected income will come in, and you'll see the switch occurring because it'll be a pull versus a push, making it much easy for you to recognize your manifested efforts.

I truly encourage you to practice my RSM technique of rewiring your mind repeatedly. You will see positive changes and a shift begin to happen within you. Don't be surprised if you notice that you start to feel or act differently, or that your entourage changes. As your inner world changes, your outer world will also shift.

"All you need is the plan, the road map, and the courage to press on to your destination."

-Earl Nightingale-

SELF-ASSESSMENT:
TAKING INVENTORY

WHERE ARE YOU NOW?

Now that you know how to take control of your mind, in the following self-assessment you will spend some time answering some other key identifying questions, beginning with "Where am I?"

I want you to take time to assess whether or not you're where you want to be. This can apply to your physical location, your career, your income, and your relationships. Are you happy? Do you experience joy in your life? Are you working in a career that aligns with what you feel you should be and are gifted at doing?

It's a good idea to grab your notebook or journal again and write out your answers as you go. You can go a little deeper by answering the questions below. Really take time to look at your life and reflect.

- Where do you live?

- Who do you live with?

- Where do you spend most of your time?

- What type of friends do you have around you?

- What type of energy and vibes are you surrounding yourself with?

- Are you spending time with people that are talking about unlimited possibilities or people that are only talking about negative things?

- Do you wake up every morning and go to a job that deep inside you feel is not in line with who you are?

- Is it out of fear or maybe necessity that you haven't changed course?

If you answered these questions truthfully and after reflecting, you feel you're not happy where you are physically from a location standpoint, in your neighborhood, apartment, country, marriage, relationship, etc., let's spend some time reflecting on each area.

I invite you to pay attention to how answering the above questions made you feel and how you feel about each area of your life.

- How do you feel about yourself?

- Do you feel happy?

- Do you feel you're missing something? If so, what?

- How do you feel about the place you're living in?

- The people you live with?

- How do you feel about the neighborhood or overall environment you live in?

- How do you feel about the work you do every day?

Answering these questions will help to show you where to focus your energy. Listen to your intuition. What is your intuition telling you to pay more attention to?

INTUITION

Intuition is that feeling you get inside of you that acts as a guide to follow. I truly believe that our intuition is a direct and divine connection with the Universal Source. It's meant to guide us.

Intuition gives you insight and ideas for your highest good. During your reflection time, your intuition might have nudged you to do some research about something. Maybe your intuition told you to research moving to another country. Maybe it suggested you train in a new field for better career options. It might tell you that you spend too much time helping others or listening to others and to put that time into your own life first.

What is your intuition telling you? What guidance are you receiving from yourself or have received that you have ignored?

Another key question to ask yourself is, "If I continue to live my life exactly as I do right now, in the same environment, working the same job, in 15 to 30 years, would I have any regrets? Here are a few other questions to help you reflect on a deeper level.

- If you knew you only had three weeks left to live, what are five things you would do immediately that would provide fulfillment and peace?

- What conversations would you have with the people in your life?

- Would you take a trip?

- Would you want to live elsewhere?

- Would you start a rock band?

- Do stand-up comedy?

- Are there areas that you feel a calling for?

- Are there people you'd want to apologize to or forgive?

When you're reflecting on the above questions, make sure you take off any limitations. Don't consider your financial situation or family commitments. Give yourself the opportunity to just daydream and see yourself experiencing the things that will allow you to get the most joy and fulfillment out of life.

Allow yourself to fully visualize and imagine what your dreams actually look like. I encourage you to go beyond just thinking about them and actually take some time to write or draw all the things that come up for you in this exercise because as we continue, these notes or drawings will serve as your roadmap and guide you toward the right next steps to take if a major change is in order.

As I shared with you in the preface, my immediate environment growing up in France was one that reflected scarcity and struggle. When you look out into the world and what's staring back at you is negativity, despair, and scarcity, it can be difficult not to succumb to these things. However, by having a vision of what I wanted to see change and knowing how I desired for my family to live, I was able to eventually create that reality.

Now that you have taken the time to get a more accurate vision of where you are and where you'd like to be, it's time to ask yourself the most important question of all. What's blocking you from making a change? Why do you feel restricted about pursuing the things you want to achieve? Do you feel you don't have enough money? Is it not knowing where to start? Is it the voice of someone close to you telling you that it will never work? What are the limitations that you keep hearing? Note them. Add them to the list of things that in your mind are keeping you from pivoting toward the direction of your dreams.

Maybe you learned not to pay too much attention to your feelings. You might believe that your feelings aren't important and as a result you don't value them. However, the change you desire really starts from within. The outer results that we experience in life a lot of times reflect what's going on inside of us. Getting a grip on your life and your external reality requires you to get a grip on your internal reality and requires you to face it. It requires honesty, and it requires courage.

The wonderful thing to note here is that you always have your best interest in mind. No matter what your relationship is with yourself or your level of self-love or self-awareness, your higher Self always wants to see you win.

YOUR RELATIONSHIPS

Evaluating the state of your relationships is also key here. Our relationships can either encourage or discourage us from being who we truly are and living a life of fulfillment and happiness. Take inventory of your relationships. Not just your family, friends, or romantic partnerships, but also your religious community, your co-worker relationships, and other community-based relationships.

- Are they loving and harmonious?

- Do you feel supported?

- Do you feel valued?

- Does your circle encourage and uplift you?

- Are your relationships primarily positive?

- Are you balanced and your true Self within your relationships?

- Do you have boundaries in place within your

relationships?

- How do they make you feel overall about your current relationships?

Now that you have a clearer picture of your relationships, you might have also received some intuitive guidance on adjustments needed. The saying goes, "You become who you surround yourself with." Even better, "You're the average of the five people you spend the most time with." Jim Rohn.

There is a lot of truth in these statements. Tony Robbins says it this way,

> *"The people you surround yourself with have an impact on your goals. Proximity is power. Learn how surrounding yourself with quality people can help you."*

Again, who you're around and what you're around can either accelerate and encourage your growth or stunt it. Just like every other area, your relationships should be aligned with your happiness and fulfillment. If you have people around you that are not serving you positively, it's important to figure out why you choose to remain in unproductive relationships.

You might fear hurting someone in a relationship. You might be afraid of not knowing how to transition into a new neighborhood, city, country or career because you may not know people and feel intimated by forging new relationships. You might feel inadequate or limited in your social skills. You might fear rejection.

Notice the pattern here. No matter what the reason is, the bottom line is that fear is blocking you. It's the fear factor that's standing in your way.

Many times, our fears are imaginary. We perceive them as real but they aren't. In the next chapter, we'll discuss how to move out of fear and how to take control of your compass. You've already sketched out a map that will help you shift and transition from where you are to where you want to be. Now it's time to learn how to get moving in your desired direction and put your plan into action.

SELF-ASSESSMENT LAYERS

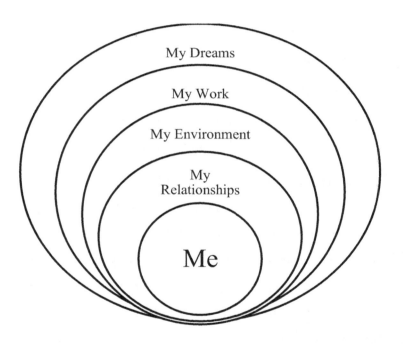

My Dreams

My Work

My Environment

My
Relationships

Me

TAKE CONTROL OF YOUR COMPASS

You now know where you are today. You also have an idea of where you want to be. The next step is pivoting toward fulfillment. I call this, "Taking Control of your Compass."

You've already completed the hardest part. You faced yourself and your reality. You looked at your situation and you acknowledged things for what they are. Then you went deeper, and you took the time to reflect on your insight and to sit with it and really feel through everything to see what needed to surface and come up for you.

Now we'll switch gears here a little and focus in on the controllable. Can you change the people around you? No. But you can change and control YOU. You can begin to take action to create change in the areas of your life where they're needed.

Focus on controlling the controllable.

I'll be completely transparent with you here. Before

I had any idea around the concept of taking control of my compass, I suffered from what we might call victim mentality. I literally thought everything was outside of my own control and that I was at the mercy of "someone" giving me an opportunity or whatever it was I needed in order to progress in life.

Going about life with this perspective dominated my thinking and kept me in perpetual negativity, so my results during this phase of my life were never what I wanted. Feeling helpless and hopeless isn't exactly motivating, and it doesn't help you attract to you what you want. It didn't for me, anyway. It also didn't help that I still had work to do around healing my self-esteem and self-worth issues.

My early beliefs about myself caused me to make a lot of excuses for why I couldn't do this or that. When I look back on it, the culprit was always someone else. I didn't take responsibility for myself, my actions, or my life, and this only made things worse.

Finally, I just got fed up with being disappointed and not really having any "real" person or thing to blame. I chose to focus on doing what was in my power. I made a list of what I wanted to change, and then I just began taking action on my list. Suddenly, as if by some stroke of magic, the results I got were the results I wanted. A lightbulb went off. That's how this strategy came about in my life. I used it repeatedly, and it worked. I want you to use it to your best advantage from now on also.

Go back over the lists you created in the self-assessment for each area of your life that you feel unfulfilled. Are you unfulfilled in your relationships, career, finances, environment, physically, or any other areas? If so, write three to five key actions that are within your control to take next to each area you desire to change.

For example, what are three to five actions you can take that will help you align better within your relationships? The action steps should focus on things you can do to see a shift towards being more fulfilled and happier in your relationships. If you're struggling with misunderstandings in your relationships, an action step you can take to help is actively working on your communication skills.

Proper communication consists of both verbal and non-verbal skills as well as listening. I will touch on this a little more in-depth in a forthcoming chapter.

After you've written out your action steps on the things you can control within your relationships, do the same for your environment in terms of your home, your neighborhood, your city, and your country. What steps can you take to begin to shift toward a healthier, more aligned environment?

Maybe that looks like researching the country or the city you wish to live in, or possibly another neighborhood in your current city. Maybe it's reaching out to your country's embassy or city hall to discuss issues that need improving to make your environment a better one to live in.

Again, think about small, key steps, you can take to start to make the shift. All action doesn't have to be drastic action, however sometimes it needs to be. You must decide which course of action you're best suited to take and most comfortable with.

However, remember it has to be a tangible action. Not just wishes or ideas. It has to be something you can actually do, now, to get to you where you want to go.

Repeat this action list for all other areas on your list. To see a change in your career or workplace, you could take steps to go back to school to further your education or look into certifications in your field or another field you wish to transition to. Maybe you want to change jobs completely. Take action by refreshing your CV or resume and putting your name out there to position yourself for new opportunities. Maybe it's creating your own business.

Whatever it is, list the key actions you can begin taking to get closer to reaching your goals.

Once you have your list of action steps around each area you're focusing on, set a date that you plan to commit to in order to complete each action. It's not enough to say, "I'll update my resume soon." It's too vague. Soon to you might be next year and that's counterproductive to you controlling the controllable.

Take time to assess, commit, and then execute.

Taking action is where many people get stuck. It's easy to be excited and pumped up about your ideas and about your updated vision, it's more difficult to actually follow through and execute the newly drawn up plan. However, this is the only way you'll be able to get from where you are to where you want to be. The map is just that, directions; it requires you to take steps and take action.

You might need someone to help you with this, an accountability partner. I encourage you to share your plans with someone you trust within your circle that can hold you accountable. Implore an accountability partner to help you stay on task within the timeframe you set to get things done. Remember, this is a benefit to you. It's for your best and highest good. It's a promise to yourself. Don't sell yourself short or let YOU down.

Many people feel like it's impossible to start to make even minor changes to their situations in order to experience something vastly different from what they're used to. However, you didn't get to where you are suddenly. It took time. It took repeated action. And guess what? You're already more than capable of the shift you want to see happen in your life.

The time is now. Decide. Use courage to act. No matter how small the action is, continue doing it daily so that you can put things in motion. Sooner than later you'll begin to see transformation happen in your life. Where you are today and where you want to be are not that far apart. Where you are today compared to where you feel you should be and how you should live your day-to-day life is missing only one thing. Action.

Taking control of your compass is really about acting on the deep feelings you have and the inner guidance of your higher Self, which is in line with your greatest happiness, overall fulfillment, and who you really are. It's really a personal commitment to yourself. You're committing to your soul guide and not your logic or conditioning based on what you think makes the most sense or that might please others.

When you take control of your compass, your

actions are in full alignment with who you believe you are and what you believe you should experience in life. Then you commit yourself to the work in order to move into full alignment with your true Self.

Remember that your life is precious. It's important for you to practice trusting yourself. You were created to live in abundance, fullness, and happiness. It's who you are. You can't use someone else's roadmap and expect to reach the destination meant for you. Intuitively, you really do know best.

TAKE CONTROL OF YOUR COMPASS CHART

I Performed the Self Assesment	I Recognize My Situation	I Commit to Control the Controllable	I've Listed my Key Actions with Targeted Completion Dates	I am Delivering on my Promises	My Life is starting to shift positively

DISCOVERING & LIVING YOUR PURPOSE

For a very long time I used to always ask myself the following questions, "What is my purpose? Why am I here? Why do I exist? What is the Universal God's plan for me?" These are all essential questions to help us uncover the truth of our existence and to dive deeper into self-awareness. The idea of living a mundane life, getting old, and dying without truly finding out who I was and what I'm here to do was once one of my biggest fears.

Throughout the years, I initially thought that my purpose was my job. I also thought destiny was already written, and I had to just go along with whatever happened, fate would decide everything for me.

However, as I experienced more of life, I realized we were all given gifts and abilities and are meant to put our gifts to good use for the benefit of all humanity. The following quote really helped me grasp and understand this with simplicity. "Do not ignore your gift. Your gift is the thing you do the absolute best with the least amount of effort." Steve Harvey

Ask yourself the following questions:

- What are three personal values that really describe my core essence?

- What do I want everyone to remember about me?

- What are three things I really enjoy doing the most on any given day?

- What are three things I do exceptionally well or naturally with the least amount of effort?

As I answered these questions for myself, these were my answers:

- Honesty. Authenticity. Solidarity.

- I would love to be remembered as someone who cared about others, who lifted up and inspired those that were down, and a leader who drove progress.

- I enjoy driving positive change. I enjoy setting out strategy and vision. I enjoy solving problems.

- I can naturally look at any business and figure out

ways to improve it.

- Leading and influencing people.

- Anticipating organizational and people's needs.

Now that you have answered these questions for yourself, living your purpose is about making the conscious decision to be in environments where you can freely express the most authentic version of yourself, while doing what you enjoy, and contributing to the betterment of those around you.

If your current situation does not enable you to do these things, then review and implement the strategies laid out earlier in this chapter to take positive steps toward changing your life and living your purpose. I know sometimes it's easy to limit yourself by thinking, "I have commitments, I can't change like that," or "I don't have what it takes."

However, I want you to remember that there is always a way. The more you're aligned to your true Self and gifts, the happier you'll be. Therefore, the Universe will start to send all the help you need to achieve your desired outcomes.

Have faith and take a step. Take five steps towards what you want, take intentional action, and the Universe will exceed your efforts by aligning things to attract toward you.

GIFTS & PURPOSE CHART

My
Essence
& Values

My
Natural
Abilities

My Gifts
& Purpose

My
Legacy

What
Brings
Me Joy?

"It is really amazing what people can do. Only they don't know what they can do."

-Milton Erickson-

MY SECOND ACT

D on't stay here. The world is bigger than where you are right now. I want you to expand and go see what's out there, son. Expand. The world is bigger than where you are." My mom used to always tell me.

Those words always resonated with me.

In high school it blessed me to join the rugby family in the South of France, which helped my personal growth tremendously. It gave me a level of structure and the sense of family that I was missing in my single-parent household. I became a part of a brotherhood and made some lifelong friends. Life opened up to me a little more.

However, I had already decided during that time I wanted to play rugby and work at a bank. To me, working at a bank was an excellent job that made good money and would allow me to provide a better life for my mother and myself. I was becoming a man and wanted to contribute to our household income. Even though I had my mind made up, inside I always felt I could do more, become something bigger, but I didn't know what that really looked like or how to pursue it.

Then the birth of my little sister Gloria-Rose brought about a change in me that's difficult to express in words. At the time of her birth, we were living in a housing project called Chateau D'eau. The day she was born, I remember holding her little body in my arms. Seeing her pure innocence. Knowing she arrived into this world in circumstances beyond her control, I made a promise to her and to myself that day.

"I will become someone great. You will never miss out on anything in life. I will always protect you."

I whispered to her as I kissed her forehead and snuggled her closer to me.

From that moment on, I had a new motivation and inspiration. I knew that my meager plans wouldn't be enough for me to make good on that promise. It was time to figure out another, better plan, more in line with who I knew I now needed to be vs. who I was.

In high school, my friends nicknamed me the Sage. They used to ask me for advice and believed me to be the wise one in the group. I never paid much attention to the signs then or to the loud voice in my head always encouraging me and helping me to see past what I could see with my eyes. Even though I always carried within me a deep feeling of wanting to help the world fight injustice. It was difficult for me to witness or know that people are suffering or being treated unfairly.

There is a memory that sticks out for me about child injustice in Africa that I witnessed personally that helped activate my desire to advocate for others. I was very young, maybe six. I had a friend named Fatou; she was like my big sister to me. She sold ice cream close to where I lived.

One day I was walking by her house and I saw her well-dressed but crying. I found out later the reason why she was in such despair. She was being forced to marry at just fourteen. She had an arranged marriage with a much older man who looked very mean. I remember how sad she was and how desperate and hopeless she seemed.

Seeing her suffer didn't sit well with me. In my core, I felt a powerful desire to act, to help her out of her suffering. However, I was just a small boy. What could I do? That's one moment that has stayed with me and it planted a seed of desire to affect people's lives for the better. "I have to do something. I will do something. I will make an impact." Those words were shouting at me in that moment, and they've been repeating nonstop throughout my life journey. This desire to help has been innate since as far back as I can remember.

Obviously, as a young boy of six, I didn't have the experience or knowledge to know what was really going or the magnitude of the situation. I just saw someone I cared about crying, sad, and in a situation that appeared to be against her will. That was enough for me to want to do something about it. Looking back, I can see that there was something else at play. Something bigger. I couldn't put a word to it. It was just a feeling that told me I'd eventually do "something" to help others.

Over the years, that same feeling has crept up again and again in many personal and professional situations in my life. Many times, early in my professional career, I felt isolated, strange, or out of place because of this sense and need to do what's right, no matter what. Especially in the world of large multinational corporations, where you encounter certain people who will not hesitate to crush you for their own success.

However, even though behavior aligned with traditional corporate culture was the path expected of me, there was something in me helping me to stay aligned to who I was, "different" on many levels, and to operate outside of the status quo.

I enrolled in business school in France and started my journey toward a bachelor's degree in business management with a finance concentration. During my last year of business school, I had the opportunity to travel overseas, allowing me to visit the US for the first time. We had a family friend living in Dayton, OH.

Until my trip to Dayton, I stayed stuck on my original life plan, not feeling I could do any better. Change for the better was still too hard to believe. However, once I had the chance to see another reality outside of what I knew, I finally felt the power behind my mother's words all those years. For two months I experienced what it meant to "expand." I learned that the world was in fact much larger than what I had experienced up until then.

I remember the first time I stepped inside of the corporate headquarters of one of the major banks. I was so excited. I dressed as if I had an interview. An African American lady was sitting at the reception desk.

"Good morning, can I help you, young man?"

"Yes miss. I want to give you my CV because I want to work here."

I can only imagine what she must have been thinking. "He can barely speak English. Is he serious?"

However, she wasn't rude, and her response was enough to ignite the fire I needed to believe in myself and the possibilities ahead of me.

"Okay. Give me your CV and I'll pass it through our channels, and we'll see what we can do."

I left the US realizing my potential. I could be more than what I thought my circumstances in France dictated that I could be. When I returned to France, all my friends actually told me at the time that I looked so different. They knew I wasn't the person I was before I left anymore. I had changed.

My last year in business school went by quickly. In the same year, I lost one of my childhood best friends and neighbor, William, tragically in a car accident. He was like a brother to me. His tragic death drove me to make the tough decision to leave my mother and sister in France and to see what I could make of myself abroad.

At first, I hesitated to leave my hometown because I didn't want to leave my mom and baby sister there without me. However, I figured I had to get out of my comfort zone if I was to change the immediate circumstances of my mother and sister living in a housing project. I felt it would be difficult for me to build any type of future if I stayed. Shortly after graduating, I moved to Dublin, Ireland to begin my MBA and a career in corporate finance.

Exposure is usually all that's needed to help us realize there are other possibilities out here for us. Oprah Winfrey once said, "You don't become what you want, you become what you believe." So, in order to believe, you have to have exposure to the possibilities.

I never heard back from the bank I submitted my resume to in Dayton. However, that wasn't the point. It was a much-needed boost of confidence of what might be possible for me. It gave me hope for something more.

When I got to Dublin, I had to overcome the obvious hurdles of the cultural and language barriers standing between me and new opportunities that I now know were out there waiting for me. I was enthusiastic and determined. My drive was at an all-time high. I interviewed for various positions. However, many times I went to interviews clueless, especially at the beginning because I didn't really understand how things were done and couldn't speak the language very well.

Time after time I got rejected. I heard no after no after no. Looking back on it now, it was a time of trial-and-error and tremendous failure. Time after time, I met failure. However, in the moment, it didn't feel that way because I had a clear picture of where I wanted to go, and I was working toward getting there with every small step.

Determined to get my foot in the door somewhere and add value, learn, grow, and show my worth, I didn't let the failures discourage me. I knew that my extra motivations were strong enough to propel me past all the obstacles thrown my way. I needed so badly to get through all the "no's" so that I could make it to a "yes." I just needed one.

I honestly feel like the Universe had put blinders on me because none of my negative feelings toward myself showed up to distract me during this time. It wasn't until I got further into my career and started progressing up the success ladder that they came back up to visit and sabotage.

After all the "no's" and having a few 'you're wasting your time" I got a "yes." A multinational company offered me a position as a senior analyst and I quickly accepted. I was able to learn, grow, and add value. It was a dream come true.

I was learning more about myself during this time. However, it was still very early in my journey and my inner workings were still a mystery to me. I was blinded by wanting to make good on the promise I made to my little sister and my mother. I was too busy proving myself to be able to foreshadow what was just beyond the horizon. Life appeared to be working for me, finally. The tides shifted in my favor, and I wanted to do everything in my power to keep them that way.

Every small step toward progress pushed my suppressed feelings of abandonment, anger, frustration, resentment, and living in lack a little further out of the scope of my reality. Surely, I had solved for them by gaining strides in my education and beginning a budding career in finance. These issues wouldn't have a reason to show up again during this time and cause me anymore suffering. I'd moved past that phase of my life.

However, when we don't resolve old issues, new ones arise to build on the old ones.

It took me time to figure this out. I would keep hitting walls. The pain kept building on itself.

Until I did.

"Knowing yourself is the beginning of all wisdom."

-Aristotle-

BOOK TWO:

MASTERING YOURSELF

"Mastering others is strength.

Mastering yourself is true power."

-Lao Tzu-

SELF-MASTERY

Self-mastery is all about being in alignment with who you are, having a keen sense of self-awareness, and understanding of your inner being. Self-mastery can apply to someone who has achieved a holistic understanding of who they are intrinsically before they decide to go out and experience the world.

To become a master at anything, you must first have a certain level of understanding on the subject. This is why we took time in Book One to unpack and get to know you and your inner workings better. Behaviors result from what you think about yourself, based on your own knowledge.

However, if who you think you are has been shaped by other's projections on you, this has likely distorted your truth and clouded your vision. You're not the sum total of the stories others have told you about yourself. They have filtered their stories about you through their beliefs about themselves, which often come with extreme limitations and bias.

Now that you have taken the time to experience yourself and build up some self-awareness, we can move into some key strategies that will help you attain self-mastery.

I came to understand the concept of self-mastery and holistic self-awareness as they related to my core personal agreements when I read the book, *The Four Agreements* by Don Miguel Ruiz. The book really resonated with me when I read it. The main ideas were the missing pieces in my life at the time.

In simple terms, the book lays out four core agreements or core rules to live by that help you stay in alignment with who you are and allow you to live in harmony both within yourself and within your world.

The first rule is to be impeccable with your words, meaning to speak with integrity. Being able to say what you mean and not using your words against yourself or others. An example of using your words against yourself would be: "I'm not good enough. I'm not pretty enough. I'm not strong enough. I'm clumsy. I'm not a kind person." Make sure that you use words in a positive and edifying way towards yourself and others as much as possible.

The second core agreement Ruiz shares is to not to take anything personally. When you get cussed out by someone close to you for no reason, when someone at work criticizes you, or you get into an argument with a stranger during your checkout at the grocery store, take nothing that's said to you personally. Don't internalize the other person's words or actions. Instead, ask yourself: "Do I believe what they're saying toward me? Is it true?"

Whatever someone does or says really has nothing to do with you. So, the answer to both questions should be, no. Their words and actions reflect their own inner reality. They aren't being impeccable with their words and instead have projected onto you their inner reality. It has nothing to do with you or how they feel about you; it is how they really feel inside about themselves.

It took me a really long time to grasp this core agreement. I remember a time when someone could make a negative remark about my character, physique, or abilities, and I would take it personally. Once they made the remark, I would think about it, wonder why the person did it, and stress myself out about something that ultimately wasn't true. Ultimately, I caused my own inner suffering, not the person who made the negative comment about me.

The third core agreement is to never make assumptions. This one was also huge for me. I remember times when I made crazy assumptions about why my boss never greeted me or why my manager never showed appreciation for my great work. I would create endless scenarios of reasons why I wasn't included in a meeting, or sometimes it could be the way a person looked at me as I was crossing the street.

The bottom line is I had no idea why things were going on and I felt the need to feel a sense of control and that's where the assuming started. The thing about making all these assumptions is more than likely they weren't true, but I had no way of knowing. So, the inner chatter continued endlessly. It further damaged my view of Self, my self-worth, and my confidence.

Again, all the negative self-talk caused me a lot of unnecessary suffering.

Making assumptions is much easier than having the courage to ask a question in order to bring clarity to a situation. "What do you mean by this?" We need to ensure we communicate with each other clearly in order to avoid misunderstandings. When you feel confused or unsure, find the courage to ask a simple question instead of assuming. This will keep you from suffering and will help the situation and the relationships vs. hurting it.

The fourth core agreement is focused on doing your best no matter what. That means that every single time you attempt something, for every task, small or large, unimportant or meaningful, you should focus on doing your best. When you do your best, you avoid judging yourself and abusing yourself with harsh words and criticism. You also don't have regrets.

Doing your best every time gives you confidence no matter what the situation or task is. Doing your best is liberating. It helps free you from the burdens of negative self-talk, self-criticism, etc. It also allows you to feel positive about the situation and you aren't as focused on the outcome, which is out of your control.

CONTROL THE CONTROLLABLE

Control the controllable. Your actions. Your thoughts. Your behaviors. Your energy. By focusing on controlling what you can control, you avoid causing yourself unnecessary suffering. Worrying about things you can't control is not a good use of your precious time or energy.

Most of the time, people naturally focus on elements outside their control. We cannot control the economy. We cannot control other people, their behavior, or their opinions of us. Spending so much time worrying, stressing, and criticizing elements outside our control only spends our energy, keeps us distracted, and gives us a false sense of control.

A better strategy to take is asking yourself, "what can I do with what I have right now?" Then take what you have and do your best to act on the situation in order to bring resolution. By doing this, you will automatically feel more empowered to act and less helpless. You'll also be acting in the best intent to get the best results. Things will come into alignment more easily and with less resistance.

For many years, I caused myself a great deal of suffering because I was not aware of these simple yet profound concepts around mastering myself. Once I discovered them and started using them in my everyday life, consciously, my level of inner suffering decreased significantly.

Essentially, they have to do with how you think, react, and operate in your everyday life and the actions you take as a result. They are within your control so again as I've stated before your energy, time, and effort is best used controlling the controllable, YOU, leave the rest to the God of the Universe.

THE TRUE MEANING OF FAILURE

Opportunity often comes disguised as obstacles."
Napoleon Hill, *Think & Grow Rich*

As I mentioned in my second act, the constant rejection should've been enough to turn me around and figure out the fastest way back to the life I knew I could obtain in France. However, each rejection gave me an opportunity to reflect and uncover a missing piece or some area I needed to work on in, order to get to the ultimate yes.

This is why understanding yourself is so important and where humility plays a key role. If you're not open to learning, improving, growing, and mastering yourself, you cut off the possibilities of success and fulfillment. Facing yourself requires extreme courage and a sizeable amount of objective honesty. It helps you to mature and grow your emotional intelligence, which I'll touch on in a forthcoming chapter. These are also skills that you will need to help you better navigate through life, your career, and relationships.

Everything begins and ends with you. Facing yourself helps you better face your obstacles. It equips you to handle whatever gets thrown your way. You become more confident because you know who you are and what you're capable of. You learn to be proactive instead of reactive, which also serves as a source of power you can use to your advantage.

Everyone goes through a season of good times, when we feel luck is on our side, when things just fall in place and seem to work out. Then the tide shifts and we begin to face challenges. The challenges feel difficult and painful. However, the one thing to understand here is that the very obstacle that appears to be a curse is really a blessing in disguise. This is the secret behind every challenging situation. There is always a vital learning opportunity that will enable you to grow and improve.

Where do you feel the most uncomfortable? Stay there. Face it. The only way is through it. By facing the uncomfortable, you'll get the lesson. You will become stronger and better because you'll have new skills.

Facing your obstacles means you'll get the answers you need to help you understand what each lesson was meant to teach you.

Once you achieve mastery at this level, there'll be a time of recovery and often new blessings before the next, bigger challenge arises that you'll have to face and find solutions for. It's part of the normal cycle of life. Only by facing the uncomfortable are you able to grow, learn, and improve yourself.

Bruce Lee said it like this:

"Be like water making its way through cracks. Do not be assertive, but adjust to the object, and you shall find a way around or through it. If nothing within you stays rigid, outward things will disclose themselves. Empty your mind, be formless. Shapeless, like water. If you put water into a cup, it becomes the cup. You put water into a bottle, and it becomes the bottle. You put it in a teapot, it becomes the teapot. Now, water can flow, or it can crash. Be water, my friend."

Be water and flow. Learn who you are. Master

yourself and exercise control over your mind, your body, your words, actions, and your reactions. These are all things you have control over.

Focusing on controlling the controllable empowers you to feel strong and capable. When you are in alignment with who you are at your core and acting in integrity and excellence, this gives you balance and inner peace. This helps you face the difficulties of life with courage and persistence because you know that everything that happens is for your learning, growth, and good. You either win or you learn.

MANAGING YOUR NEGATIVE EMOTIONS

Being able to control your thoughts is another key to accessing the path to success. So how do you control your mind on a daily basis? How do you navigate negative emotions, self-doubt, and other negative influences? That's the challenge we all face every day no matter where we are, who we are, or how successful we are. It's important that you get a better handle on your thoughts and emotions so that they are working for you and not against you.

When you have moments where you experience strong, negative emotions or self-doubt, depending on the basis of these thoughts, they can be paralyzing. In the moment, you can really feel hopeless and not know how to get out of that counterproductive thinking.

When this happens, it's imperative you take a moment to breathe through it and remember you're in charge of your destiny. The negative beliefs and emotions arise when you suddenly forget you are the master of your life and of your journey. The moment we feel like our destiny is in the hands of someone else, a manager or boss, significant other, our kids, or family, we enter into an emotional state where we lose control.

When we feel a loss of perceived control, our natural survival instincts kick in and activate the negative thoughts and doubts in our minds, which generate a bunch of "what if" scenarios that most likely won't occur. "What if I lose my job? What if my significant other cheats on me? What if I don't have enough money to start over?"

The underlying cause is the belief that our destiny, our life journey, whatever goes on in our lives is really in the hands of something else, a person or an entity, and not in our control. Refocusing on your goals and your journey without thinking about the "what if's" and the fact that the outcomes are out of your hands, will help.

The question to ask yourself in the moment is, "Will worrying about all the "what if's" actually help me right now?" No. Because it's very unlikely that the scenarios you're playing out in your head will ever actually happen. What you have to do is focus on controlling the controllable. You can control how you feel in the moment. You can control your beliefs around the fact that you are in charge of your life. You can also make choices and any necessary adjustments in the moment to change your outcomes.

When dealing with other people, it's really in your best interest not to assume. The negative chatter in your mind could cause you to project onto others your negative thoughts, and this will almost always cause you suffering. The scenarios in your mind are not real. They haven't occurred and are unlikely to occur.

Again, the only way to get through challenges is to go through them. There's no way around them, no shortcuts. Trying to avoid them just causes more pain. Do your best to seek a quick resolution so you can turn off any negative thoughts and reduce the amount of suffering they cause you and others. When facing tough situations always ask yourself, "What is the right next step for me?" then act on it.

"The purpose of pain is to move us into action.
It is not to make us suffer." -Tony Robbins-

Negative emotions and self-doubt also cause stress. Stress results from not taking the time to address the things in our lives that really bother us. Many people describe their everyday lives at work as being stressful. However, what is the actual cause of the stress many people experience in their jobs?

If you've ever said, "I'm stressed at work." Why are you stressed? Let's take a moment and dig a little deeper. Is your job itself stressful? Do you enjoy what you do? Do you need less responsibility? If you don't enjoy what you do. You might actually like being busy, but just not enjoy what you do. The fact is not doing what you enjoy on a daily basis causes your stress, not the job itself.

Addressing the stress in this situation would mean being honest about your need to explore other opportunities within the company, perhaps in another department or you might realize it's not the department but the company or industry. Stress comes from not addressing the actual cause behind the things that bother us.

A technique I learned and have used throughout my own journey is asking myself, "what's the worst thing that can happen?" Instead of stressing myself out and making myself sick, physically, mentally, and emotionally, I stop, breathe, and think through how to best confront the actual cause of my stress and suffering.

"What's the worst thing that can happen if your manager doesn't like you? What's the worst thing that can happen if you get fired? What's the worst thing that can happen if my significant other breaks up with me?"

Once I asked myself these simple questions and thought through the scenarios, I could see that nothing really life-ending would happen. If I lost my job, I would search and eventually get a new job. I would eventually heal from any heartbreak and find love again. I would learn how to cope with whatever situation actually happened. I would address it and come up with a solution. That's the best way to deal with the negative thoughts on a daily basis. Take their power away.

Know that no matter what you face, you'll always find a solution and persist because it's your nature.

Fear is not real, it's just a perception of reality that we have the power to change. Have the courage to face fear straight on. It will be tough at times, of course, but maintain your faith and take small actions to move forward in spite of any perceived fear.

THE IMPORTANCE OF SELF-CARE

In addition to understanding and mastering yourself and your inner workings, I want to take a moment to emphasize the importance of self-care. You need to focus more of your time on actually taking better care of yourself. You are invaluable. Taking care of your mind, both conscious and subconscious, your thoughts, your body, and your relationships are all key in excelling in life and winning in each area of your life.

Where you live, your surroundings, the people you spend the most time with, what you eat, and how you spend your time all contribute to your overall well-being.

Even if you can't pack up and move today, you can continue to practice the techniques I've already laid out for you to help you reverse the negative self-talk. You can continue to tune into the things that bring you joy and fulfillment and make sure you're spending more time doing those things on a day-to-day basis. You can remove yourself from toxic people in your life to protect your new positive energy, your conscious and subconscious mind, your body, and your dreams from negativity and discouragement.

Remember that listening, hearing, and feeling negativity repeatedly is how you learned the behaviors you now need to unlearn in order to reach your path of enlightened success. Those beliefs got embedded in your subconscious and those beliefs become your thoughts, actions, and behaviors. They have ultimately become your results.

Make sure you monitor your thoughts as much as possible from now on so you're able to check any old thought patterns that try to creep up to throw you back into old negative behavior. If you catch yourself spending a lot of time thinking or repeating to yourself why you can't do something, that you're not good enough, or about what others think about you, make sure you acknowledge it. Then take a deep breath and repeat the opposite of the negative thought.

For example, if I hear the thought, "Kevin, you'll never be able to do that." I just say to myself out loud the opposite, which is, "I can do everything I desire to. Everything will be fine."

Once you consciously counter the negative statement with a positive one, make sure you change your body position or posture because your body positioning and posture affects your positive or negative emotions.

What I might do is, if I was sitting when the negative thought arose, I might get up and walk around, or go get a glass of water, a cup of coffee, or go for a walk outside. The important thing to remember here is to change your physiology as it plays a key part in your emotions. Doing this regularly will help properly anchor the positive counter-thoughts and boost your overall feelings of well-being.

Over time, you'll notice that the average number of thoughts in your mind will change to more positive ones. This is also why doing things that make you happy is so important. When you do what you truly want to do, it raises your positive energy and helps you easily create and maintain a higher vibration. Mainly because you're feeding your soul and allowing yourself to experience pure joy. When this happens, it decreases the likelihood of your mind being overrun by negative thoughts.

Pure joy activities for me include swimming, walking along Lake Michigan, going out on the weekends to have a nice breakfast with a good cup of coffee, and training in Muay Thai Martial Arts. It's walking along the streets in my neighborhood in the evening to reflect on my day's journey and to clear my mind.

Spend some time now thinking about what you really enjoy doing. You. Not just what your family likes to do, your kids, or your friends, but you. Like on the plane when they say, "secure your oxygen mask first before assisting others." Remember that your personal fulfillment will give you enough fuel to serve others.

Once you create your list of pure joy activities, begin doing the things on your list for the pure enjoyment you will get out of them. You shouldn't consider any of these activities a waste of time. When you don't make time for yourself and your enjoyment, it takes a toll on your body, mind, and emotions. The toll of pouring from an empty cup will negatively impact your relationships as a result. Always give yourself permission and take time to recharge.

Another part of a good self-care routine is a daily meditation practice, which we already covered in an earlier chapter. It's crucial that at the end of each day you completely clear your thoughts and the energy collected throughout the day through meditation. It can be a quick one or you can go deep, whatever feels good to you and helps you clear out your thoughts and feelings. Because what we don't clear comes back up repeatedly.

These are a few practical actions you can incorporate into your daily routine. These are in addition to the classics, which include sleeping well. There is a myth out there that says that in order to be successful you have to sacrifice sleep. You may believe that successful people wake up at 3:00am or 4:00am. Well, that's not true of every successful person.

It's important that you forge your own path to success, which means figuring out what you need and doing that. Sleep is necessary to your overall success. Your body needs rest as well as your mind in order to be alert, effective, and productive while you're awake.

Another self-care classic is eating right. Ideally you want to eat things that are healthy. I won't push you into eating only a plant-based diet. However, the more you eat plant-based, the better you're will feel and the more energy you'll have to help you sustain yourself through all of your day's activities. Drinking enough water is another classic self-care tip.

All these actions are the keys to maintaining the beautiful engine, your body, that you're blessed to live in. Your body is your real home while living this life. It's your temple. Treat it well.

MANAGE YOUR TIME WELL

Managing your time is also in line with your overall self-care. Time is one of your most important and greatest resources. As I stated in the last chapter, giving yourself permission to take time to recharge ensures that you're looking, feeling, and acting your best. How you spend your time is a direct reflection of whether or not you're adequately taking care of you.

Once you spend time, you can't get it back. Make sure that every second, minute, and hour you have every day, you spend effectively, and in alignment with your goals and dreams. We all have 24 hours in a day. How we plan and effectively manage these hours plays a vital role in achieving success in all areas of our lives.

Examples of Poor Time-Management

- Spending time on other people's priorities and putting your own goals and dreams aside consistently for prolonged periods of time (months/years).

- Choosing busyness over productivity. Being busy doesn't equate to progress. Focus on quality over quantity.

- Overcommitting yourself to numerous back-to-back meetings and tasks can negatively affect your health, mental wellbeing, and relationships. Creating balance is important.

- When you focus too much on doing things for others and completely lose touch with yourself and your needs.

- Spending your time watching TV, gossiping with people, or complaining about things you can't control.

- Dropping your important priorities in order to please others' needs and their agendas.

- When you believe your success will come from pleasing others instead of consciously driving your agenda and being guided by your higher

Self.

Examples of Maximizing Your Time

- Recognize that your time is limited therefore highly important.

- Make a commitment to manage your time effectively and make it a priority.

- Know how your physiological clock works (are you a morning person or night owl, once you find out, embrace it! Don't force yourself to wake up at 4am, when you know you're at your best late in the evening.

- Plan your day ahead and set positive intentions before starting it.

- Have a clear agenda, set your intentions, outline key deliverables, and stay focused on these in every meeting.

- Disconnect when it is time to and only compromise on it for rare exceptions.

Every successful person manages his or her time carefully and with great focus. These are some of my personal tips:

Before Going to Bed

Before going to bed at night, I set my intentions (written or mentally spoken) for the next day. "Tomorrow will be an incredible day where I feel energized and inspired. I will make significant progress towards my projects and I will achieve success in collaborations with my partners. I'm so grateful for this."

Morning Routine

- I wake up at 7am, breath for few minutes, then I practice Tony Robbins Priming Exercise

- I go for a quick run (30 mins), followed by a quick workout, then a quick swim.

- Once I'm back home, I meditate for about 25 mins before preparing for work or going to enjoy a nice breakfast if it's the weekend.

Work Routine

- I'm very selective about the meetings I attend, focusing my mental energy on meetings that add value. I ask myself, "Is this meeting a 'must have' or 'nice to have', if it is a 'nice to have' I decline or delegate it.

- I schedule meetings that will require my full mental focus or high IQ meetings (solving a problem, discussing significant opportunities, brainstorming, etc.) from 8.30am until 12pm.

- From 2pm until 6pm, I schedule catch up or update meetings, selectively.

- I block time on my calendar for 'Visioning' sessions, where I sit, reflect, and strategize, about 30 minutes daily.

- After 7pm, I commit to not engaging in any work activity (checking emails, taking calls, etc.). On the weekend, I completely switch off. This is key for me to recharge and make sure I'm present when spending time with loved ones. I also take time to work on personal projects.

Outside of Work Routine

- I schedule my personal activities and projects in

my personal email calendar, that includes vacations, nights out with friends, my workouts, and other activities.

- It's important to keep business and personal items separate. This helps you maintain your boundaries around not working during your personal time.

- I prioritize my personal time based on the activities that are important to me and that make me happy. My personal time is sacred.

Begin spending time each day, paying close attention to how you use your time. If you need to make any adjustments at home or at work, start by trying out some of the ways I mention above to help you prioritize your time better. As you implement the above tips and stay consistent with them, you will start to see tremendous growth around realizing and fulfilling the goals that truly matter to you.

MY THIRD ACT

My excitement and enthusiasm for finally being able to get a foot in the door at a great company, helped to absorb a lot of the learning pains and turbulence that I experienced early in my career. Even though it felt like things got off to a slow start, initially, after landing my first position, the time flew by. Within only a few short years, I went from being an analyst to moving into a management role. During that time, I gained invaluable connections professionally and even had the opportunity to work in New York City, which was another dream come true.

I was optimistic and stayed engaged, always looking for ways to grow professionally and add value. My personal life was also in good shape during this period of my life. I had found someone who I cared for deeply and it seemed like for once, everything was actually working as it should be. I continued to ride the wave, and the water felt great. However, without my paying attention or maybe because I didn't want to acknowledge the possibility of anything going wrong, I neglected to recognize the shifting winds.

The wave started getting a little choppy and before I knew it, what had been smooth sailing, quickly became a shipwreck. It happened so fast, there was nothing I could do to control it or reverse course. I had to ride it out and wait for things to settle, before I'd be able to sort it all out and salvage what remained.

After the storm waves finally subsided, there was literally nothing left for me to salvage from the wreckage. I had lost my job at a company I loved and thought I'd have a long future with. I'd also lost my relationship. I would literally have to start over from scratch again.

In addition to my newfound money problems, my self-esteem was crushed. Dark thoughts and old feelings, since buried and forgotten about, decided it was the perfect time to emerge and show themselves relevant again. I questioned everything, myself, my worth, my purpose. I wanted so badly to be accepted and valued.

I thought that I would find that value and acceptance in my career, in titles, and in the things money could buy.

"It's all your fault. You weren't good enough." My inner voice screamed at me. The little boy I once was that never had the safety, security, or love of a father spoke. His voice, cracked and afraid, was painful to listen to. However, he refused to be silent through this ordeal. The issues I left unattended were now echoing in my head and in my heart. I felt like giving up entirely.

I spiraled down into a deep tunnel of depression. Anger, feelings of abandonment, loneliness, and worthlessness were the exact opposite of the highs I experienced on the success train I had just got knocked off of. I got lost in my own debilitating internal chatter of remembrance. Once again experiencing the feelings that resulted from my father not being in my life, the separation from my mother as a young boy, feeling like

I wasn't deserving of love, success, acceptance, wealth, stability, and happiness. I wallowed in self-pity and idleness, feeling lost.

I wrapped my identity up in too many external things, my career, the things that money could buy me, and the fleeting sense of approval you get from what you're able to help others attain. The thought of going back to nothing terrified me. It was too much to handle. I didn't know how to cope. I felt ashamed and inadequate.

At first, I thought I should move back to France to be with my mother and sister and give up on my aspirations and the promise I had made to myself and my baby sister at the time of her birth. How in the world was I going to ever "become" something I was clearly not? A success. The last thing I wanted to have to do is return to them empty-handed. However, I could see no light at the end of the tunnel.

It was my turn to pick up the phone. The only person in the world that could help me out of this state was my mom. This time I needed her help, wisdom, and guidance.

"Everything happens for a reason, Kevin. One step back allows you to make a leap forward." Her voice resonated through to my core being.

I let her words soak in without responding, envisioning her arms wrapped around me in a comforting embrace.

"Don't settle for just anything though. Now you can create the life you want. What do you really want now?"

"I don't know."

"Well, think about it and listen to your heart."

Shortly after our conversation, a recruiter contacted me about a position and about my career aspirations. Again, I was told to consider what I really wanted to do next and where. It challenged me to use my imagination to create the next chapter of my life.

Thinking back to that period of time, the hardest thing for me to do was to think positive and see beyond the gloomy, but temporary circumstances. Looking back, I wasn't out of work very long. Once the recruiter contacted me and I really took time to listen to myself and figure out what I wanted to do next, I realized my desire to have more upward mobility, travel around the world, and discover my Asian roots.

Once I was clear about what I wanted next, it was like Paulo Coelho describes in his masterpiece, *The Alchemist.* Everything conspired to support and usher me toward the direction of my dreams. I asked for exactly what I wanted, then suddenly the next position I received was a promotion. Within a eighteen months I received another promotion and accepted a position to move to Singapore, reporting to the Regional Head of Asia Pacific, to drive the profitability of the company's markets in Asia Pacific. Those markets included Japan, Singapore, Malaysia, Indonesia, Australia, New Zealand.

Talk about being beyond over the moon. A year before you couldn't have convinced me that the world wasn't ending and that I would be where I was just a brief time later. The opportunity came after there was room for me to receive it. I had to get clear about what I wanted. I had to show some resilience and some toughness. I had to push through the darkness and choose to focus on the slither of light, which at the time were my mother's words of wisdom. I had to choose not to give up on myself and settle for a life I didn't really want to live.

The lessons I learned during that time opened up the door to my paying attention to the issues going on inside of me that I still needed to resolve.

The biggest challenge in my time of darkness was figuring out how to get my inside world to match up with the outside image of success and happiness I had found again within the realm of my career. If I didn't, all the money in the world wouldn't be enough. There would still be gaping holes of emptiness left by feelings and beliefs that I knew weren't valid, but that I didn't know how to resolve on my own. I also acknowledged my need to get some understanding around how to better handle myself when faced with hostility and ongoing challenges.

This is where my journey inward really began. Once I moved to Singapore and was thriving in my new position, I sought help with working on my internal struggles. I desired to grow as a person and to invest in not only my professional development but also my personal growth. I sought to become better, whole, and an example of how to lead others in a way that helps everyone attain their goals and be their best selves. I didn't want to make the same mistakes of the examples I had early in my career as a manager myself. I wanted to be able to help and not hinder, to elevate and not tear down.

However, in order to do this, I had to tear down my own insecurities, dismantle negative self-talk, kill off feelings of doubt and fear, and put an end to my own personal suffering. Once I decided to improve myself, everything conspired to work to point me in the right direction.

I met wonderful teachers across many disciplines and fields of intellectual and spiritual knowledge that shared of themselves and their learned lessons and experience. I also made significant investments in coaching, talk and hypnotherapy, seminars, and programs to help me go further and deeper. I am still a work in progress because I believe that the work that is me is still growing and changing every day.

I'm so grateful I didn't give up, and that I took personal responsibility for my life, even though at the time it felt much easier to just quit. It didn't look like it in the moment, but the opportunity I really wanted was wrapped up and waiting for me to push past the disguised misfortune.

The act of picking myself back up was also a blessing because I needed to show myself that I had what it took to make my dreams come true. I needed to prove to myself I could actually do and be what I said I wanted to do and be. It was to be the best I could be. I told myself that I would be a VP before age 30 because I knew that that is a tremendous accomplishment for anyone to achieve no matter what their background.

However, even with the intense growth, I still knew

that I needed to learn more about myself and more about others, as well as to develop my emotional intelligence. I needed time to mature and grow as a person before I would get there, but it wouldn't just happen because I wanted it to. I would have to be intentional about working to become the person who lived the life I wanted to live.

During this time, my values shifted. I no longer attached my worth to my career or material wealth. I realized I'd have to value myself above everything else because that's something that can't be taken away from me if I lose all else. I still wanted to be successful and meet my goals, but I needed to be reminded that at my core, I am people-centered and care about helping others. I also decided that I didn't want to choose between this or that, I wanted to be able to operate holistically, balanced, and in harmony with everything.

I rejected the notion that you have to choose, sacrifice, or settle. I decided that health, wealth, and success were attainable for me in all areas of my life. It was only a matter of me figuring out how to build properly on this new foundational truth. Once I began building on the more solid foundation of truth, it was much easier to find the balance in all the other areas of my life. Although it hasn't been easy, ultimately, I have worked to establish harmony and have found an overall balance.

Looking back, I needed the heartbreaking experiences I went through early in life and in my career to prepare me for what has been rapid acceleration and opportunity to live out my dreams. My muscles were getting formed and shaped, so to speak. I needed all the feelings of inadequacy and for my childhood issues to trigger me because they showed me what I needed to work on internally.

I no longer needed to muffle the cries of my inner child. I needed to embrace him and nurture his healing. I needed to solve for my early years of negative programing and reprogram myself to align with what I wanted to create so that all my channels were communicating on the same frequency.

Ultimately, all of my challenges allowed me to learn the lessons I used to create a new mode of leadership within the business world. I needed every single lesson. All of it worked together for my overall highest good.

Even having insight and direction on where I was headed and a roadmap on what I needed to work on, I still had a long way to go before I would begin to see the fruits of my inner work. It would take the same time, effort, commitment, and consistency that I poured into my career aspirations.

Honestly, it took even more. There were no shortcuts. Even with the help from my teachers and guides, the road required the courage of a lone journeyman. It required me to walk it alone. Things didn't get easier so-to-speak, but I was less affected by negative situations because I had a better understanding of who I was and how to handle the people in my life.

The more progress I made along my healing journey, the more resistance I felt trying to push me backwards. Obstacles still showed up at every turn.

Frustration and fatigue set in on many points along the way. I learned that the only way to heal is to surrender and let go of what no longer serves you. It was a matter of me having to choose between holding on to the history of myself and making room to become who I was destined to be.

The external battles continued, and so did the internal tug-of-war for a time.

Until I did.

"Every adversity, every failure, every heartache
carries with it the seed of an equal or greater benefit."
-Napoleon Hill-

BOOK THREE:

UNDERSTANDING OTHERS

UNDERSTANDING OTHERS

Our lives are filled with various types of relationships. Friendships, family, romantic partners, business partners, colleagues, strangers. Not a day goes by without you being in contact with others and needing to function successfully within your interactions with other people. Now that you have a much better understanding of who you are and how to achieve self-mastery, it's also important to have a good understanding of others.

A large part of achieving success in all your relationships is to know what others' need and how their actions are motivated by these needs. Based on that knowledge and your observations, you can adjust (flex) your communication style in order to influence others. This doesn't mean risking your authenticity, but rather it helps show your ability and understanding of one-person inner dynamics in order to communicate effectively, build relationships, and drive consensus.

In 1943, American psychologist, Abraham Maslow

published a paper in the scientific journal, *Psychological Review,* on motivational psychology that outlined what's considered the best-known theory of motivation in human beings. He later published, *Motivation and Personality,* where he fully expands on his well-known theory, *Maslow's Hierarchy of Needs.*

He illustrated the hierarchy as a pyramid where the basic needs of a person are at the bottom and each level represents different needs. Each level represents a person's motivations or developmental growth phases as they progress. Once the person's basic needs are met, they move on to the next level and so on, which is considered the natural progression of human development and advancement.

Our basic or physiological needs are at the bottom of the pyramid. Maslow concluded that every human being no matter what their race, age, or culture has the same basic needs critical to their survival. These needs include air, water, food, shelter, sleep, clothing, sex, and the ability to remove waste from our bodies.

The second level of the pyramid focuses on safety

needs. A person's need to protect their health, resources, family, emotions, property, morality, their bodies, and their employment motivates them.

The third level focuses on love and belonging. Since the person's basic and safety needs are met, they're now ready to focus on their needs as it relates to their relationships. Friendships, family, and sexual intimacy fall under these needs.

Moving up the ladder, the fourth level are needs around a person's esteem. Self-esteem, confidence, achievement, respect of others and from others, as well as status, recognition, and freedom.

Finally, after reaching the first four levels and satisfying each need, an individual at the top of the pyramid develops the need for self-actualization. The person wants to be the very best they can be. This is the level where they're able to tap into their highest creativity and work to fulfill their highest needs.

Maslow believed that each level on the pyramid needed to be achieved and fulfilled within the person before it motivates them to move up the pyramid and focus on higher pursuits.

Why does this matter? If a person's basic needs are not met, it's difficult, if not impossible for them to be able to care about fulfilling their need for self-actualization, which is at the top of the pyramid and the ultimate goal or motivator for people's development over time.

I want you to be mindful of this basic yet crucial information on human behavior. As you interact with people, notice how they manifest their situation based on what they say or believe. The whole idea of mastering the understanding of others is for you to be aware of what drives human behavior in order for you to flex your style and optimize your approach as needed in order to influence others positively.

EMOTIONAL INTELLIGENCE

E motional intelligence also plays a significant part within our relationships and our understanding of ourselves and others. Emotional intelligence is the ability to identify and manage one's own emotions, as well as the emotions of others within relationships wisely and empathetically.

I can remember back to a time when the concept of emotional intelligence was foreign to me. I never paid attention to how my emotions played out in my life, at work or in my personal relationships. I had a very one-sided view of things and didn't embrace or find comfort in expressing my emotions when I felt them. If someone told me something I didn't like, I reacted based on feelings of anger.

Unexpressed anger turned into resentment because oftentimes I internalized or took what they said or did, personally. I didn't try to understand where the other person was coming from or their side of things. I dismissed other's feelings because I dismissed my own.

This type of behavior didn't get me the results or deep connections I valued and desired. It also didn't align with who I was because I naturally feel deeply connected and moved by people. I took on the façade of what I thought was acceptable in terms of how a man should act, feel, and behave, without regard to who I was. This is the exact opposite of emotional intelligence.

However, this changed when I began working with a master executive coach, who first introduced me to the concept of emotional intelligence and what motivates most people and why. I could then see myself and others through the lens of empathy and compassion. As a result, my career and relationships improved. It was an important missing piece of the puzzle because for the longest I couldn't figure out where the disconnect was happening.

Ultimately, we all have the same basic needs, but as the Maslow hierarchy illustrated, we might be at different levels of obtaining those needs and this is what drives us and determines where we put our focus.

Besides having different motivations, we also have unique personalities, and different ways of processing information. As a result, it's important that we as individuals, take the time to learn how to better relate to and understand each other. This is the role that emotional intelligence plays.

According to American psychologist Daniel Goldman, there are five key elements that play a role in emotional intelligence. These are self-awareness, self-regulation, motivation, empathy, and social skills. To be a master influencer and have the best chances of achieving success in this lifetime, you need to have a mix of all these tools.

Self-awareness is the ability to understand your moods, your emotions, and what drives you to act in ways that ultimately affect yourself and others. Self-awareness helps you to keep yourself in check. Your moods, emotions, and actions shouldn't affect other people negatively. Self-awareness gives you the insight to control or redirect your disruptive impulses and moods before they pose a problem.

Self-regulation deals with your ability to exercise self-control, hold yourself accountable for doing what you say you will do, and also showing a level of calmness and composure under pressure. Ultimately, it's your job to make sure you have the capacity to manage and self-regulate yourself because the moment you lose it in front of people, you immediately lose influence and it makes it hard for you to rebuild that once it's lost.

Motivation, in terms of emotional intelligence, deals with self-motivation. It's the powerful desire and passion that drives personal achievement. It's also the ability to be optimistic, even in face of failure. Motivation helps you sustain your initial level of enthusiasm in order to achieve progress over time and obtain your goals. This ensures you're able to see what you start through to completion, which is necessary for success in life because it often takes many attempts and much persistence to reach the finish line.

The fourth element of emotional intelligence is empathy. Empathy is the ability to understand someone else by putting yourself in their shoes. Empathy is being able to observe how someone feels, what they're going through, and being able to adjust yourself and your way of communicating or behaving in order to match the level of compassion appropriate for the circumstance at hand. Empathy is critical for leaders and others responsible for managing or leading teams or companies. Empathy helps others know that you care about their needs and well-being.

Lastly, the fifth component of emotional intelligence is social skills. Being able to communicate is an essential component to managing relationships, building networks, energizing collaborators on projects, and building rapport with people in every walk of life. Meeting people where they are is essential to cultivating great social skills. Being able to listen with patience and with the goal of understanding helps you connect on a deeper level with others. Asking questions when you need clarity is also a part of communicating effectively. Your body language should show that you are interested and attentive. Great social skills also include celebrating others and their value and contributions.

Showing genuine appreciation for others, no matter who they are or what position they hold in your life, can sum up emotional intelligence. Success in your lifetime is intricately intertwined with your ability to create and sustain viable relationships in all areas of your life.

PERSONALITY PROFILING: DISC

Personality profiling is the next step in understanding others better. There are numerous personality tests you can take to find out your type. I was introduced to the DISC method on my journey, so I will refer to this method below. The assessment measures your patterns of behavior based on your tendencies and preferences.

It's important to understand that each human being is born with a specific personality type and while they might have a mixture of traits, there will be one personality trait that's dominant compared to the others. The DISC model focuses on four types of personalities. These include Dominance, Influence, Steadiness, and Conscientiousness.

- People under the **Dominance** profile are very direct, results oriented, very strong willed, and quite forceful.

- People under the **Influence** profile are very

outgoing, enthusiastic, very optimistic, highly spirited, and lively.

- People under the Steadiness profile are quiet, very even-tempered, accommodating, very patient, humble, and tactful.

- People under the **Conscientiousness** profile are very analytical, quite reserved, very precise, very private, and very systematic.

Why is this information important? Many years ago, I used to wonder:

- Why is my manager so direct with me? He doesn't like me.

- Why does that person keep asking me millions of questions in meetings in front of everyone? She's trying to make me look bad.

- Why is that person so quiet and always observing me? I may not be good enough for them or they are plotting something, they want to get rid of me.

As you can see, for many years I was making false assumptions that led to suffering unnecessarily! When

I learned about the power of understanding personality profiles with a master executive coach in Singapore, I understood that everyone is naturally built a certain way. Often, our interactions with people are never really personal, but just the natural way a person communicates and interacts with others. Knowing this ahead of time will help you stop taking the words and actions of others personally. You'll now be able to operate from a place of understanding the dynamics of each person you are in a relationship with and can adjust your approach to ensure better communication, which is beneficial for all parties.

In order for you to influence people, first: you need to understand what personality profile is most dominant for you. Second, you need to understand the profile of your key relationships (at home, at work, or in your community). Third, based on that information you need to be able to flex your style in order to influence them.

I have a steadiness personality. In the example above where my manager was very direct with me, I learned that he fell under the dominance profile. Keeping in mind that my dominant personality is steadiness, I knew that my interactions with him had to be brief and direct in order to match his natural way of communicating.

Personality profiling is not about changing who you are and not being yourself. No. The key is how to drive progress and the outcome you wish to influence by mastering the skill of communication. You can read more in depth about the DISC model by visiting https://www.discprofile.com/what-is-disc/overview/.

INFORMATION PROCESSING: NLP

Neuro-linguistic programming or NLP for short is a psychological approach involving studying strategies used by successful people and applying them to reach a personal goal. It relates to thoughts, language, and patterns of behavior learned through experiences.

Everyone processes information differently. Based on observation, I adjust my techniques according to the environment and the people, allowing me to connect faster and deeper within my personal and professional relationships. There are three core ways most people process information.

Auditory. The auditory person learns better by hearing spoken information. For this person, in-person learning, listening to speeches, live presentations, and audio books will be the best ways of getting information to them. They prefer to hear from you and have a conversation vs. receiving a text or email, for instance.

Visual. The visual person learns better by being able to see information in order to process it. Most people are visual. Articulating information to them is better done through written or drawn presentations, graphs, pictures, flowcharts, symbols, etc. They need to be able to see what you're talking about in order for them to grasp it.

Kinesthetic. The kinesthetic person learns by doing. They are best able to process information by touching it, interacting with it, and getting a feeling of what's being done. Fewer people will fall under this category. You'll want to incorporate something interactive and hands-on in order for them to fully comprehend what you're talking about or showing them.

Why is this important? Knowing how people process information allows you to be proactive in how you communicate with them. You always want to do your best to meet people where they are and to be as clear as possible in your communication. Doing so will enable you to get the results you want faster and with the least amount of effort. You won't have to try so hard or risk miscommunication.

If you know someone processes information visually but you choose to communicate with them over the phone, over and over, you will feel as if they don't get you or what you're trying to say, which is only because you need to adjust your approach, not your message. Writing them an email or going to speak with them in person would be a better approach.

The same thing applies to sending an auditory person a long drawn out email explaining something. They'd prefer to have a conversation with you and actually hear what you have to say, be able to ask questions, and hear how you respond to them. You will lose them by sending a long email to try to convince or explain something.

It's important for you to observe how the people around you process information. If you have a friend who always says, "Hey, let's talk or I want to hear you out." They're auditory. Your boss might always tell you, "Show me your ideas. I need to see it clearly in my head." He or she is visual. Your co-worker might respond to things by saying, "I need to work through it, or I need to sample it before I decide." This person is kinesthetic.

Knowing how each person processes the information given to them will help you connect and align with them in order to accomplish what you're trying to achieve. It may seem like the process is very involved, but it's not. It's actually really simple. Now that you know how to listen for cues, it's only a matter of paying attention and adjusting your approach to suit their needs.

MOTIVATIONAL FRAMEWORK

In 1960, David McClelland developed the *Achievement Theory of Motivation,* which revolves around three critical aspects, the need for Achievement, Power and Affiliation. His theory pointed out that regardless of age, sex, race, and culture, each person possesses and is driven by one of these needs. These motivations influence and drive their behaviors.

The Need for Achievement: A person motivated by this need is driven by the desire of accomplishment and notable successes. If you are an athlete, it is the need to become an MVP or play for the most prestigious teams. If you are an actor, it is the need to win an Oscar. If you are an employee, it is the need to be promoted and recognized for your work.

The Need for Power: A person motivated by this need is driven by the desire of having control or authority over a person, organization, or institution, with the need to enhance their reputation and self-

184

esteem. There are two subtypes of power, Personal Power (It's all about me over everyone else) and

Institutional Power (I want to be powerful in order to drive progress and change for the good of everyone).

The Need for Affiliation: A person motivated by this need seeks to have close interpersonal relationships with others. They enjoy working in groups and also creating friendly relationships. They like collaborating with others instead of competing with them, and they usually avoid high-risk situations and uncertainty.

The Need for Avoidance: A person motivated by this need seeks to avoid situations and people with which they have, or expect to have, unpleasant experiences. These avoidance motives include fear of humiliation, fear of rejection, fear of failure, fear of success, and generalized anxiety.

The key here is to identify someone's current dominant state of motivation, understand it, and know how to adjust your communication approach (to take it into consideration) in order to influence them or build relationships. For instance, if you are managing a team and you identify a team member motivated by power, you want to make sure you give them opportunities to lead tasks and projects. If you identify that achievement motivates your manager, you know the key for her/him is to talk about topics that are contributing to achieving major outcomes.

The secret to this is to listen to the person. The words they use will help you identify their most dominant motivational need at that moment. Obviously, one motivational need may change over time and you may notice how being able to help someone meet their motivational needs will allow them to evolve.

APPLICATION

Understanding others requires you to have a good deal of emotional intelligence and the ability to be unselfish, which we covered earlier in this section. It also requires that you listen to understand, not just to respond. Using the tools of personality profiling, NLP, and motivational frameworks will help you get the most out of your relationships and your communication with others; whether it's at work, with your family or spouse, with your friends, or in your community.

All these strategies help you become a better communicator. Ultimately, communicating is at the core of every interaction and relationship. Lack of proper and effective communication is at the cause of discontent, misunderstandings, and personal suffering.

Using these techniques is not about manipulation or trickery. It's about communicating holistically and reaching desired outcomes for all parties.

It's important that as you navigate through life and enter into relationships with people that you understand what level they're on because this will tell you where their focus is. Their focus is the driving force behind their behavior and what they perceive as their priorities in life at that time. As I mentioned, the key to driving progress and reaching your desired outcomes or to influence others positively happens by mastering the skill of holistic communication.

It might take you a little time before these skills become natural to you. However, in order for that to happen, it will take you making a conscious effort every day to apply this knowledge in your normal interactions with others. Once you do, you will see how great of a positive influencer you become and how you'll be able to improve your relationships in the process.

BOOK FOUR:
BECOMING A MODEL LEADER
& INFLUENCER

"The challenge of leadership is to be strong, but not rude; be kind, but not weak; be bold, but not a bully; be thoughtful, but not lazy; be humble, but not timid; be proud, but not arrogant; have humor, but without folly." –Jim Rohn-

LEADING AND INFLUENCING PEOPLE

Leading and influencing people is a natural part of life. We all have to lead or influence people at home, at work, in our social circles, basically in all areas of life. Now that you have a better understanding of how people work and what motivates them, the next step is learning how to develop solid leadership skills.

The act of leading is universal. When I was learning about the information I'll share with you in this section, I approached it from a business perspective. So, I'll be explaining the frameworks around leading and influencing people in a business context. However, you can use them just as effectively within your personal interactions and relationships with others in order to improve your results.

So, how do you become a better leader & influencer? Dale Carnegie's, *How to Win Friends and Influence People* was a fundamental part in my learning the foundations of basic social interaction and communication, especially because of the social, cultural, and language differences from country to country as I navigated my way through my career and industry. I believe schools across the world should make his book recommended reading at a very young age because it would help children develop more holistically.

Here are some fundamental techniques to use in your core interactions with others.

- Do not criticize or condemn people. Show sincere appreciation.

- Become genuinely interested in other people.

- Smile, it's basic, but true.

- Remember that a person's name is the sweetest and most important sound in any language.

- Be a good listener.

- Encourage others to talk about themselves.

- Talk in terms of the other person's interests.

- Make the other person feel important and do it sincerely.

- The only way to get the best of an argument is to avoid one. That's very critical.

- Show respect for the other person's opinion. Never say you're wrong.

- If you're wrong, admit it quickly and empathically.

- Try to see things from the other person's point of view.

- Be sympathetic to the other person.

- Always begin conversations with praise, honor, and appreciation.

- Call attention to people's mistakes indirectly.

- Talk about your own mistakes before criticizing the other person.

- Ask thoughtful questions.

- Praise every improvement. Use encouragement.

- Make faults seem easy to correct.

- Offer correction in the form of a suggestion and

make the person happy about doing what you suggest.

Before I learned about this skill, resentment and conflict riddled my personal and professional interactions with others, but I never knew why. By learning Dale Carnegie's approach and how to better communicate with others both verbally and non-verbally, I realized that changing the words I used or the way I used them in the smallest way meant the world to people and could cause different, more favorable reactions.

Relationships of any kind are essentially very fragile. A minor mistake in the way you talk to someone or the tone you speak in or the words you use can make or break it. Once broken, it takes time, attention, and a lot of work to repair.

Being able to positively regulate your emotions while communicating with others is an effective way to connect quickly. People react to emotions. Displaying your emotions helps you show why something is important, how it will make a difference, why you're passionate about it, or why you feel sensitive about it. It's important to show emotion in your interactions with others from a healthy, mature place, however. When you're communicating it's also important to be able to prove and convey the facts as well as show you're knowledgeable or have the background to prove your argument.

Communication also consists of non-verbal factors as well. How you look plays a part in effective communication and how others perceive you and what you're saying. Other people will try to conclude whether you look trustworthy, confident, kind, or knowledgeable based on how you present yourself. Your body language will dismiss or confirm their doubts. How you stand, where your eyes go, what you do with your hands, whether you perspire, etc.

Start paying attention to not only what you say, but how you say it and what your body conveys as you speak. Make sure all three are in alignment with the message you're trying to convey.

SIX LEADERSHIP STYLES

What type of leader are you? Your leadership style also plays a role in effectively leading and influencing people. Daniel Goldman, with Harvard Business Review outlined six basic leadership styles that I want to share with you below. See which ones fits you best.

The Visionary: Inspires others by believing in their own vision. This leader is empathetic and people-oriented, sharing with others how their contributions will impact the overall goal or dream. Visionary leadership is appropriate to use it when a change is required because change requires presenting a new vision with a clear direction or path to follow.

The Coach: Is a great listener and helps others identify their own strengths and weaknesses to contribute to the overall goal. This is a leader who counsels, encourages, and delegates responsibilities. Coaching leadership is best used to help motivate employees to improve performance by building long-term capabilities.

The Affiliative Leader: Someone who is great at promoting harmony, boosting moral, and solving conflicts. This leader is friendly and empathetic. This leadership style is best used to motivate people during stressful times or to strengthen connections.

The Democratic Leader: A leader who is really good at listening. A team player, a collaborator, and an influencer. This style is best used to build support or consensus or to get valuable input from employees.

The Pacesetting Leader: Has a powerful urge to achieve or demonstrate results. This leadership style illustrates a low level of empathy or collaboration, and they are more impatience and more of a micromanager, concerned with numbers, facts, and are metrics driven. This style is best used to get top results from a motivated and competent team. Especially when you need to show progress, growth, or achieve an outcome on a tight timeline.

The Commanding Leader: Is someone who is commanding, controlling, and threatening. An extreme micromanager. This style is the least effective. It generally drives away talent and contaminates everyone's mood because it's toxic. This style is best used during a critical crisis, or to deal with a problem with an employee, or at the start of a turnaround situation in the organization or project.

Prior to learning the in-depth characteristics of the different styles of leadership, I didn't know there were so many styles. I thought the word leader or leadership was equal to only the commanding style.

Professionally, I've worked under all six leadership styles and after moving up the corporate ladder, I've also had to implement some of them myself in order to fit the context of unique situations and based on the different people I was working with. Some styles worked better than others in order to get results.

The important thing to understand here is that in order to influence and lead people, we have to be able to change our leadership style depending on the circumstances we're facing and the people we're leading. Knowing the different styles gives you an advantage and the ability to adjust as needed in order to achieve your goals. Remember, the key here is to stay fluid, authentic, and genuine to your true Self. This will help you win over people and progress on your path to success and fulfillment.

Your ability to use appropriate leadership styles correctly is the first step in getting the results you desire, no matter what you do for a living or what the situation is. This is a component of results-based leadership. You have to be the best you can be as a leader in order to move everyone towards organizational results. As a good leader, you're able to use your personal tools to equip and enable your team to be successful.

A good, effective leader provides the team with all the tools they need to be successful, which creates a positive climate within the team and organization. Creating a positive climate cultivates increased employee engagement. A positive climate leads to people engagement. Therefore, the other people involved will be happy and more invested in what they do. They'll be willing to go above and beyond what's asked of them.

When done correctly, this leads to increased customer engagement. All that goodness will materialize in serving the customer well. As the customer engagement level increases, the results are achieved, and success will be indicative.

Consistency is key here because being consistent helps build your value and also helps others feel more secure with your leadership and your ability to lead them. This is an effective way to build trust. In all relationships, whether business or personal, building and maintaining trust is essential to the success of the relationship.

No matter what leadership style you use, in order to be effective, it's important that you as a leader create a vision and plan that you can use to implement change. Creating a vision helps you communicate clearly and effectively why change needs to happen, what it entails, and how it will be implemented. It will highlight the benefits that the change will have on the parties involved.

Once the vision is well-communicated, you can move into a change in behavior. It's important to empower others to act and accept the vision. Essentially, you'll need the support of other's in order to make the vision happen.

Show your appreciation at every turn in order to keep your team motivated and wanting to continue through to the end.

CONFLICT MANAGEMENT

As you learned in the last section, everyone comes from unique situations with varying backgrounds, points of view, and motivations. When you manage or deal with a group of people, there will be a reason to know how to manage conflict. Managing conflicts is also key in being an effective leader and influencer.

Let's say you are in a situation of conflict within a group of people, the best conflict management approach would be to show assertiveness and empathy while taking in all points of view and displaying a collaborative approach. It ensures synergy between both parties while keeping you neutral and focused on the solution.

Here is where not taking things personally and being impeccable with your words come into play. It will take you being a master of yourself, your emotions, and your tongue in order to deescalate the situation vs. make it worse. Always focus on solving the issue at hand. Don't take sides, don't take things personally. It's never personal. Stay neutral and don't allow low-level energy to cloud your judgement. A synergetic approach is key in order to diffuse emotions and start to focus on resolving the issues or conflicts.

Remember that effective communication includes speaking calmly and with respect, listening to the other person's view, and being attentive and respectful as you listen. It's a dialogue that requires calmness, empathy, patience, and a desire to be understanding to all other parties.

Managing conflict has to do with reaching a mutual agreement with everyone involved. The easiest way to reach agreeable terms is by identifying all the commonalities between the parties in conflict. Even in conflicts, people possess similar interests or concerns and generally do want to see a positive outcome. It's just a matter of making sure everyone is being listened to, heard, and understood.

Allow people to share their needs and what's important to them because this information will reveal the source of the conflict and lead to viable solutions.

Lastly, make sure there is a give-and-take kind of approach to the solution. Each party will gain something based on their stated priorities and what's important to them, this will ultimately determine the take-aways. This minimizes the possibility of the issue arising again or for it to still feel unresolved.

Once this is done, it's a matter of making sure all parties involved get what they were promised, and that it's done in a timely fashion according to the stipulations laid out in the agreement. Make sure everyone agrees and is in alignment with the resolution before making things final and acting on the plan.

STORYTELLING & AUTHENTICITY

One last point in leading and influencing people is storytelling. Storytelling is an actual skill set. Storytelling helps you become a stronger and stronger communicator. It allows you to present information simply and can be used to build arguments, teach lessons, or to persuade.

Use storytelling to relate to people on a deeper level. However, don't just use your words. A good storyteller uses more than just their words to make a story great. They use animated facial expressions, hand gestures, body language, variations in voice tones, and even the audience to create a lasting impression on their listeners.

Stories also allow people to fully grasp your points better than other methods of communication. Sharing your personal story or journey with others is powerful because it helps to connect us to what makes us human and essentially shows us, we're one with each other. Your story has the power to help spark transformation in someone else's life.

Telling someone what they should and shouldn't do or how to live is not very effective in helping them positively change their lives. However, being able to tell a story and illustrate lessons learned from a personal and vulnerable space allows you and others to heal. It allows you to create a connection that is difficult to achieve any other way. It also is the only way to truly be authentic. Every time you share your story with someone else, it helps you become better at it.

Sharing our stories allows for a healthy level of humility and interconnectedness to be felt and experienced. It also helps you stay away from sounding judgmental or arrogant, which will aid you in getting your point heard and received. It's important to learn the art of storytelling. Use this art to influence people and to help change you and others for the better.

LEAD BY EXAMPLE

Always remember that the best way to lead is by example, which is important as you journey forward. In order to continue to evolve into higher states of consciousness and to become a powerful leader and influence people, it's important that you continue to develop yourself.

There is always work to do on yourself. We are never a final copy. There is no finish line. Ask yourself every six months, every year, where am I? Where do I feel I need to improve? What new skills do I want/need to learn to become better? When asking yourself these questions, be very honest and humble about the things you have to do and then make the commitment to do them.

Every six months to a year, make sure you do an inventory of areas where you feel strong and areas where you feel need improvement and commit yourself to constantly working on yourself. This ensures you'll stay in a state of mastery, your skills will remain relevant. It also ensures you don't become complacent. Things are constantly evolving and it's important to always stay up to date, stay on track, and stay in line with the latest advancements.

You lead best my embodying the best leader. Being that person and then giving others an example of what it looks like, sounds like, acts like.

People are more likely to follow you when you're not all talk, but when you are the embodiment of what you are talking about. This is what inspires people to not only listen, but to also follow you and emulate the model leader you're showing them how to be.

"You were brought to this planet, sent here
by a greater power to deliver something that we need.
God created everything with gifts.
You are a package sent to Earth to deliver
a gift to your generation."
-Dr. Miles Munroe-

MY FOURTH ACT & BEYOND

I truly believe committing to personal development is one of the greatest and most beneficial investments you can make in life. It means you're making an ongoing commitment to expand your knowledge base, skill set, and level of self-awareness. You're equipping your mind, body, and soul with what it needs in order for you to progress and achieve remarkable success throughout life. A lot of personal and professional development went into my being able to reach my goal of making VP by the age of 29.

Moving to Singapore was a significant turning point in my life, not only professionally but also personally. As I mentioned earlier in the book, I was first introduced to the practice of meditation while roaming around a Buddhist Temple. I was also introduced fully to the concept of executive coaching and other methods of self-improvement by the Head of Asia Pacific at the company I worked for. It was the end of the workday, and he and I were the last two people in the office. As he packed up to leave, he casually mentioned,

"I need to leave now. I have to meet with my coach."

Surprised and taken off-guard, I replied, "Coach? A coach of what?"

"My Executive Coach."

Dumbstruck, I asked, "What exactly does an Executive Coach do to you?"

He kindly paused packing up to explain.

"You see Kevin, an Executive Coach is someone with a lot of experience in the field you're in. Working with them helps you learn and foster a deeper understanding of business and leadership concepts and saves you years of trial and tribulation before you can figure these out on your own. For example, how to show leadership presence, how to manage your time, how to manage conflicts, your first 90 days in a new job, etc. The most successful people in business work with coaches or do a lot of outside training to learn new concepts or strengthen areas they need to work on."

Fast forward. After that conversation, I asked for a referral and I began working with some of the best coaches and mentors in my industry. I also started attending seminars and trainings in order to learn, gain, and improve on the skills I needed to continue to reach my goals. This saved me so much grief and time. It would have taken me years to figure out some of the same things I learned from someone who had already dedicated years of their life to master a particular area.

Since that conversation, every year I take time to do a SWOT analysis on myself. SWOT stands for Strengths, Weaknesses, Opportunities, and Threats. A SWOT Analysis is a technique for assessing these four aspects. Usually it's used by businesses in the startup phase, but I have adapted it personally as a way for me to identify external and internal factors that I need to work on. I like to see how my strengths, weaknesses, opportunities, and my threats change over time.

Once complete, I try to seize more opportunities to display my strengths. I also begin working on any weaknesses and threats. One of my prior lists included the following items:

- Overcome public speaking anxiety.

- The need to improve my speech clarity.

- Time management.

- Improve my leadership skills.

And for each one of my identified weaknesses and threats I research all the trainings (online, in person, free, paid) I can do to learn from the best in these areas. This ongoing investment in myself has fast-tracked my ability to reach my goals and has sped up my personal and professional progression overall.

Once I continued to pursue the goal of making VP by the age of 29, I realized I needed the push in order to do what it would take to reach my full potential in life and ultimately help others do the same while still relatively young. I also needed to fast track my growth and learn how to flow with life while integrating all the knowledge I received from my own hard-learned experiences.

I needed to try out different modalities in order to see what worked and what didn't. It forced me to have certain conversations and introduced me to different books, people, and processes.

Over the course of my journey, it took some time to realize that ultimately my drive and motivation to push through every roadblock and obstacle was fueled by my desire to attain happiness. Early on, I thought happiness had to do with money, titles, things, and status.

However, as I've grown holistically and got in touch with myself and who I am at my core, I define happiness differently. It's not as tangible as I once thought it was, it's subtle and has more to do with your perspective and interpretation of life than it does with life itself for me. The ultimate end goal is being able to live your life to its fullest and in happiness.

Happiness is that feeling when I wake up and know I'm not alone, regardless of whether I have my family or other people around me. I feel the presence of the Universal God. I can look at the sun, the trees, my surroundings and be there in the present moment, peaceful and in gratitude for life. This makes me happy, just being surrounded with a level of energy that resonates with who I am.

I'm a naturally positive person and knowing that my friends, family, and the people closest to me are vibrating with the same energy brings me joy. I love this and it's a really good feeling.

I believe fulfillment is answering the calling of my soul and my soul calls for learning, inspiring others, and sharing everything I know so that other people can benefit. It's the next level after happiness. Achieving happiness is necessary in order to attain fulfillment.

This is where I am now. I've been able to reach the goals I set for myself and I'm constantly creating new goals to give me the opportunity to continue to learn, grow, and experience life and my potential at its fullest.

In the same way that I've worked to attain my goals professionally, I'm equally committed to healing the lingering effects of the suppressed feelings of abandonment, anger, frustration, resentment, and living in lack had on me as a young child. I no longer have to muffle the cries of the hurt boy I once was. He's now peaceful, joyful, and content. He is healed, whole, and thriving. Helping me enjoy the journey, not just endure it.

I stayed with the same company I was working for in Singapore for six years and received four promotions. The last one was to VP of Finance USA and I moved to Los Angeles where I worked for over two years before transitioning to another company in Chicago, which has been home since then.

One thing that's been consistent throughout all my different career and life transitions is the fact I'm just as committed now, after achieving a certain level of success, to both my personal and professional development as I was when I was chasing down my very first career opportunity, trying to get my foot in the door.

Every day I work on me. I do what it takes to be the

person who lives the life I desire to live. I study, meditate, pray, read, seek, and ultimately always find what it is I need because that's how it works.

All of these things are just as natural and a part of my life as breathing. I understand that practice is the key to mastery. I would like to get to the place of complete mastery someday. That's another goal I'm working toward achieving. In the meantime, I will continue to use all I've learned to be an example of what's possible for others to follow.

The beauty of it all is how much overlap there is in using the techniques and methods in your everyday life. It goes to show that everything is in fact connected and that the more you improve and get better as an individual, the more you help others do the same, if only subliminally.

As I continue to journey onward toward my unlived dreams, I honestly feel like this is only the beginning of the work toward my dream of sharing my knowledge and leading by example through the act of storytelling. I plan to make a larger impact and leave a legacy of good once I'm no longer here. I want to know that my life meant something, and that I helped and inspired others to be courageous, impactful, and free.

The rest of my story is still being written. Stay tuned!

"Change the way you look at things and the things you look at change." -Wayne W. Dyer-

A NEW VISION OF LIFE

We're all a part of God's Universe and were sent here to deliver our gift to our generation. We owe it to humanity, to each other, and to ourselves.

Each one of us, without exception, has hidden talents and gifts that are unique to us. Regardless of what they are, our gifts feel natural, effortless. When we display them, we feel fulfilled and happy. When we feel stressed, unhappy and feel that nothing seems to work right in our lives, that means that we are not in alignment with our true desires and calling.

I believe most illnesses are rooted in us not being in alignment with ourselves. The word disease or dis-ease to me means that our bodies, minds, and spirits are out of whack so to speak and are reflecting our inner world of chaos and strife.

When we feel dis-ease (mental, physical, or emotional) it's important to work on getting things back in alignment to avoid illness. When we are aligned and feel good, we glow and our aura shines.

It doesn't matter if your gift is to cut hair, sing, help cure people, educate children, drive buses, or lead great organizations, we must endeavor to find out who we are, discover our gifts, and cultivate them so they can emerge and expand.

You are unique, there is no other copy of you in the world, be you and as you allow yourself to expand and be true to you, you will be true to Life.

HOW TO MANIFEST

First, you must take care your body, mind, and spirit. Taking care of these three aspects of yourself is key in order to manifest the life you want to achieve.

Our Spirit feels incredible when we are in line with our inner desires and calling. The best way to connect to your Spirit is to hear and feel it by going within, through meditation, prayer, moments of silence, and any other practice that brings calmness. Your Spirit responds to you through intuition, images, chills, and other subtle signs.

Your mind is fueled by positive environments. Whatever you deem to be beautiful, peaceful, or exciting and when you continuously gain new knowledge it helps you to expand and to grow mentally.

Our body feels good when we nourish it with healthy food, adequate hydration, exercise, and care. It's our vessel throughout this journey and we need to take care of it properly. Our environment plays a key role too, as our body feels positive or negative energies, which affect our health.

Secondly, we live in a world where we must understand the fundamental Universal Laws as we navigate through life. The behavior of our Mind, Body and Spirit (conscious or subconscious) directly connects and exchanges with everyone around us and the Universal Laws that are always in motion. Below I have listed twelve of the most important laws along with a brief explanation of how they work.

Law of Divine Oneness

The law of divine oneness states that everything is

interconnected. Beyond our senses, every thought, action, and event connects to everything else. We are all created from the Universal God, and that means we are all part of one another.

Law of Vibration

The law of vibration states that everything is energy. The more we vibrate feelings of love, appreciation, and gratitude, (which are very powerful vibrations) the more of those same vibrations the Universe will send back to us. The same goes for sending out negative feelings based on fear, limitation, and anger. You will receive negative energy in return. The famous philosopher, Confucius, sums it up beautifully, "He who says he can, and he who says he can't are both usually right."

The Law of Action

The law of action states that our actions should match our thoughts and our dreams. One small action taken can make a world of difference in your life. A lot of times our dreams, thoughts, and plans don't get acted upon. We wish for things to happen in our lives, but unfortunately many times we don't take the necessary actions to manifest our dreams and goals. Standing still is the best way to continue to go nowhere. Speaking in the language of your wishes and dreams is only the first step. The next powerful step is action, which will lead you to obtain your definite desires.

The Law of Cause & Effect

The law of cause-and-effect states that with every action you take there will be a reaction. The reaction may or may not be visible to you. It can come back in different forms. The more you take positive action expecting nothing in return, the more you will see positive results.

The Law of Compensation

The law of compensation states that you're compensated at the level of service you provide to the Universe or humanity. Ralph Waldo Emerson's book,

The Law of Compensation, is a must read to get the full grasp of this law. You can look at many successful people and we can connect the one thing they have in common with each other, they are all adding tremendous value to people or being of service to many through their businesses, careers, or brands. A few examples of people who are reaping the benefits of the law of compensation are Oprah, Les Brown, and Tony Robbins.

The Law of Attraction

The law of attraction is probably the most famous of the twelve laws mentioned here. The law states that like attracts like. It's important that your vibration is positive so that you're able to attract to you the equivalent. The real secret here for you to realize and act on is that you're always magnetizing to you what you are, not what you want. Once you really get this truth, it will allow you to make shifts that will ultimately change your life and your relationships for the better.

The Law of Perpetual Transmutation of Energy

This law states that on an energetic level, everything in the universe is constantly evolving and

225

changing. Every action is preceded by a thought, with thoughts themselves having the power to manifest in our physical reality.

The Law of Relativity

This law suggests that we are inclined to compare things in our world, but in reality, everything is neutral. Relativism exists in all things, and in the end, meaning comes down to our perspective and perception. The law of relativity states that nothing is either good or bad until you compare it.

Law of Polarity

The law of polarity states that there is always an equal positive side to every negative situation. Everything in life has an opposite; good and evil, love and fear, warmth and cold. The key is understanding these are all two sides of the same coin.

Law of Rhythm

The law of rhythm states that what goes up has to come down. You have day. You have night. You have success in life; you have failure. You'll experience joy and you'll sometimes experience sadness. There's a rhythm to everything. Cycles are a natural part of living life. Everything is subject to change, and that helps things grow, it adds depth, and it maintains balance.

The Law of Gender

The law of gender has to do with the masculine and feminine energy that exists in all things. Achieving your own balance between masculine and feminine energies can help you live more authentically. The yin and the yang are opposites that need each other for balance, and they tend to complement each other.

Knowing and applying these universal laws will help you tremendously as you continue to advance on your enlightened journey to success and fulfillment.

Learning them were key to my being able to transform

my life. The more you understand these Universal laws and live in harmony with them, the more effortless and successful daily life will feel. Integrating them into your life is more about understanding and conceptualizing them in a way that makes sense to you as you begin to see how they play out and work in your life on a daily basis.

CONCLUSION

As we conclude of our journey together, I want to take a moment to encourage you to keep going. This isn't the end. This is really a new beginning for you. You've read, worked through, and hopefully already started using a lot of the key information I've shared with you during our time together. You now have the tools to transform your life and reach your destined and personal definition of success and fulfillment.

Now that you know what you want and have a clearer picture on how you can pivot from where you are, it's time to move closer to alignment. You're in control. You're in the driver's seat and only you can stop you. However, you also know the areas that need your attention and how to work through doubts, fear, stress, anxiety, and anything else that is not in alignment with your true Self in order to overcome any past or future blocks.

I want to remind you that no matter what you are facing, what you've had to overcome, what your background is, or who you are, you are worthy, capable, powerful, and able to attain your goals and dreams. It's important that you be positive, patient, and loving with yourself throughout your continued journey. No two journeys are the same. You'll need to make a commitment to continue working through these strategies and methods in order to fully integrate them into your life for lasting change and positive transformation.

I didn't write this book as a quick fix. It's a companion book, meant to be there for you to reference and go back to, time and time again, as needed. Revisit the chapters and techniques as often as necessary to get the results you desire.

Nothing will happen overnight. It took me years of consistent practice, diligence, perseverance, and starting and stopping, in order to get these principles firmly rooted into my life. I'm still in process today, working, learning, and growing. You are still in process.

Take everything a day at a time. Pay attention to how you feel, what you're thinking, why you're thinking it, how you react to things that you view as challenges or obstacles. Know that in every moment, no matter what, you're always in control and you can always pivot and make a choice to act in a way that gets you realigned on your enlightened path to success and fulfillment.

However, now that you are more fully awake, there is no going back to sleep. There is no returning to the way you've been or spending precious time doing things that are misaligned with your purpose and the higher vision for your life.

You have the plan, the blueprint, the success formula. Now it's time to work it. You already have a head start because you took the time to get the information you lacked. Know that as you continue forward on your journey and continue to level-up, there will be new challenges that will arise. Also know that the key principles I've shared with you throughout this book will continue to work for you as you progress over time.

The strategies will remain relevant. As you practice them daily and they become second nature, you'll continue to build on your confidence and increase your positive energy, which you can use to further attract the things you desire.

As you deliver your gifts to humanity, realize that you live in an amazing world and you cannot compromise on being happy Now. Do your best to live in the present moment. Be conscious. Be unapologetic about your personal development, your happiness, and your self-manifestation.

Living is not a choice of being this or that. Success in your career doesn't mean scarifying relationships or having an unhealthy body because you're too busy. In fact, you can achieve everything together and in harmony. You can be very wealthy, healthy, caring, giving, and passionate about your hobbies and social activities. You should seek to achieve maximum success in all areas of your life by going beyond the conditioned mind of our modern society.

Don't allow it to limit you in any way. You don't need to make sacrifices and live in perfectly labeled boxes. Choose differently. Choose authenticity. Choose fulfillment.

Life is precious. Do. Be. Live your life to the fullest NOW.

CLOSING MEDITATION

Let's close with a short meditation.

Bring your attention to the present moment and take three deep breaths. Breathing in through your nose and out through your mouth. On the third exhale, please repeat within:

"I'm beautiful. I'm unique. I'm loved. I matter. I'm significant. I unleash my gifts to the world. I am becoming the best I can be. May my legacy make this world a greater place to live in. I'm grateful to me. I'm proud of me. I deserve to be happy, inspiring, and successful now. Thank you."

Once you've concluded your meditation, take a moment to show gratitude to yourself for your courage and commitment throughout this journey.

Remember that life is beautiful. Life is Love. Continue to do the work to find out who you are. Be who you are now. Lift those in need. Share forward.

Manifest your gifts. Be happy and joyful now.

Ultimately, these are the keys to the enlightened path to success and fulfillment. It's your choice to choose them for yourself, every day that you're blessed with breath in your body and the ability to make a fresh start. Remember to listen and tune into the voice within. Spend time with you and nurture yourself. This helps you align with your truest and highest Self. There's only one of you on this planet. Remember that we are all connected, and your realized Self is the best way to heal and elevate the collective consciousness.

Everything you need, you already possess. You don't need to search outside of yourself for the keys. The keys are within you, waiting to be discovered and used for your and other's highest good.

Everything is one. You are complete and whole. You came here a finished work. You only have to remember who you are and operate consistently from that truth and you be able to live your unique version of enlightened success and fulfillment in every area of your life as only YOU can.

"There is no passion to be found playing small –
in settling for a life that is less than the one you are
capable of living." -Nelson Mandela-

ACKNOWLEDGEMENTS

First, I want to thank the God of the Universe.

I'd also like to say a special thank you to my mother, Chantal Mackaya, my little sister Gloria-Rose Mackaya, and my entire family.

Thank you to all the teachers I have met and learned from throughout my journey and to the ones I have yet to meet.

Thank you to author and poet, C. Nzingha Smith, my writing partner, for taking this journey with me and helping me make this book what it is. I wouldn't have been able to complete this project without you.

Lastly, a huge thank you to you, the reader, for taking this journey. My biggest dream is that this book will have a permanent place on your nightstand or bookshelf, close by and always ready to be referenced for encouragement and direction as you continue forward on your path to Enlightened Success.

With Gratitude & Love.

ABOUT THE AUTHOR

Kevin Mpambou Do Dang is an accomplished, innovative, and gifted, global business leader with a wanderlust spirit and heart for helping people. His professional career and love for travel have taken him all over the world, being able to call Africa, France, Ireland, Singapore, and the U.S. home at some point along his journey. Since a child, he has had the rare gift of being able to tune into other's needs. This sparked a passion for a selfless approach to fostering success not only for himself but for the companies and countless peers he's worked with over the years.

Through speaking, coaching, and mentoring he empowers others to improve their lives holistically. In both his personal and professional life, he acts as a bridge for harmony and cooperation when interacting with people across diverse cultures to achieve the best mutual results. He leads with both compassion and understanding for humankind. This approach helps others hone in on their abilities and succeed.

As an author, Kevin's main goal is to help illuminate the potential of others through the life lessons and many renowned teachings he's learned that have propelled him from the projects of France into the corporate C-Suite all by the age of 35. "The more people know about the ways of winning in life, the greater our world is going to be."

When Kevin isn't in the boardroom or seeking out new travel adventures, you can find him practicing Muay Thai Martial Arts, boxing, or meditating to help him master his mind and body. Kevin is also an NLP practitioner, speaks French, Spanish, and English, and enjoys staying connected to his younger sister in France via video games. He currently lives in Chicago, IL.

Made in the USA
Coppell, TX
28 March 2023

14865760R00134